THE
COMPLETE BOOK
OF
CAT
CARE

THE
COMPLETE BOOK
OF
CAT
CARE

JANE OLIVER

CHARTWELL
BOOKS, INC.

Picture credits
(Abbreviations key: R = Right, L = Left, T = Top, C = Centre, B = Below, A = Above))

ARDEA, LONDON : 76; /John Daniels: 4, 12BL, 12TR, 19, 44, 72; /Jean-Paul Ferrero: 6, 14B, 29, 60, 61, 71
Bruce Colman Ltd: 33T, 64, 74; /Mark Boulton: 34; /Thomas Buchholz: 40; /Jane Burton: 11, 18, 25, 27, 32T, 36, 45, 47, 48T, 49, 52B, 58, 70, 84, 93; /Eric
Crichton: 10, 42; /Bob Glover: 57; /Dr. Rocco Longo: 82; /Fritz Prenzel: 12TL; /Hans Reinhard: 7, 8, 9, 13, 14T, 31, 48B, 52T, 54, 73; /Kim Taylor: 15;
/John Topham: 38; Gunter Ziesler: 43
Marc Henrie: 20, 21, 23, 32B, 66
The Photographers' Library: 35, 41, 78, 95
Spectrum Colour Library: 22, 30, 33B, 39, 50, 68, 69, 81; /D.E. Lennon: 67
ZEFA: 17, 24, 75, 79, 86

Every effort has been made to trace the copyright holders and we apologize in advance for any unintentional omissions. We would be pleased to insert
the appropriate acknolwedgement in any subsequent edition of this publication.

Cover pictures
TL: Bruce Coleman Ltd/John Cancalosi
ACL: Bruce Coleman Ltd/Hans Reinhard
BCL: Bruce Coleman Ltd/Dr. Rocco Longo
BL: Bruce Coleman Ltd/Bob Glover
BC: ARDEA, LONDON/J.M. Labat
TR: Bruce Coleman Ltd/ Hans Reinhard
ACR: Bruce Coleman Ltd/Hans Reinhard
BCR: Bruce Coleman Ltd/Fritz Prenzel
BR: ARDEA, LONDON/John- Paul Ferrero
Front flap: ARDEA, LONDON/ John Daniels
Back flap: Bruce Coleman Ltd/Steven C. Kaufman

Published by Chartwell Books
a division of Book Sales, Inc.
Raritan Center
114 Northfield Avenue
Edison, NJ 08818

This edition produced for sale
in the U.S.A., its territories
and dependencies only.

Copyright © 1994 Parragon Book Service Ltd

ISBN 0-7858-0133-2

Printed in Italy

Designer: Sue Michniewicz
Line illustrations: Pond & Giles
Editor: Alexa Stace

CONTENTS

Chapter 1
MAKING THE RIGHT CHOICE

Cats are handsome, elegant animals with an independence of spirit that makes them fascinating and rewarding pets.

Though they will never provide the slavish devotion of a dog, they are capable of deep attachment to an owner

who understands their needs and can provide many years of satisfying companionship.

One of the most intriguing qualities of the cat is that only a thin veneer of domestication overlays its basic wildness, so that it can turn from a cuddly bundle of purring contentment to a savage hunter in a matter of minutes.

Over recent years, while the reputation of dogs has taken a knock, cats have gained in popularity. On a practical level they are clean, quiet, relatively undemanding, and they adapt just as easily to a tiny flat as to a country estate. It has even been demonstrated that cats are good for our health: the soothing action of stroking a cat lowers blood pressure and pulse rate and cuts the signs of damaging stress.

THE CAT FOR YOU

Many owners give less thought to acquiring a cat than they would give to choosing a dog - and some live to regret it. The cat may be part of the family for the next 18 years, so you need to give some thought to the type of pet that will fit best into your household. A little planning in advance will ensure that you make the right choice.

You may assume that you want a kitten: not only will it be cute and comical for the first few months, but you will be able to train it in your ways from the beginning. On the other hand, it will need a lot more attention and cost you more in veterinary fees than an adult cat. A kitten may be a good choice if you already have other pets, as it will be seen as less of a threat and will readily accept its place in the household. However, if you have young children, an adult cat is a more sensible choice: it will be better able to avoid clumsy little feet, and the over-eager arms of your toddlers are less likely to end up with scratches. A mature cat may take longer to settle in - though cats are far more adaptable than is usually supposed - but it will be better suited to an elderly owner, or a household where everyone is out at work during the day.

OPPOSITE: *A pair of male ginger kittens stay close during the early days in their new home.*

ABOVE: *Charming though they are, kittens are not always the most sensible choice, particularly if you have small children.*

If your cat will be left alone a good part of the time, if you plan to leave it in a boarding cattery while you go on holiday or keep it permanently indoors, then you might consider obtaining two cats at the same time. When you take two kittens from the same litter, the move is far less traumatic for them, they are already playmates and used to sleeping and eating together and you will not need to separate them for a quarantine period. Even if you want an older cat, it is not difficult to find two friends both in need of rehoming; cat rescue charities often find that they have to split up pairs of cats used to sharing a home for years, in order to find them new owners.

WHICH BREED?

Most cats are 'moggies' belonging to no particular breed; less than 1 in 10 cats in the U.K. has a pedigree. Moggies are generally more robust and easier to care for, besides being considerably cheaper to buy. On the other hand, obtaining a pedigree pet is less of a lucky dip: you will have a good idea of its adult looks and to some extent you will be able to predict its temperament - though all cats are individuals and any pedigree can surprise you by developing a character quite unlike its relatives.

The choice of breed depends very much on personal taste, but it is wise to consider the general characteristics of a breed, as well as its winning looks.

The most popular breeds include:
SIAMESE: slim and elegant, with a wedge-shaped head and pale-coloured body with points in a darker colour. They are

ABOVE: *A black and white persian is beautiful to look at and most are sweet-natured.*

ABOVE RIGHT: *A seal point siamese has the classic good looks of Egyptian cat imagery.*

outgoing and demanding with strong personalities and a need for plenty of warmth. Siamese can be so noisy that some catteries refuse to accept them.

BURMESE: less highly strung than Siamese, they have slightly stockier bodies and come in many colours: chocolate, blue, lilac, red and cream. They are playful, loving and extremely fastidious.

PERSIAN: the most popular of the long-haired breeds, with a silky coat, cobby body, broad head and round eyes. They are intelligent, sweet-natured and placid, adapting well to life indoors. Everyday grooming is a must or their coats will become hopelessly tangled. They sometimes suffer from respiratory problems.

RUSSIAN BLUE: lithe, sleek body with plush, blue-grey fur and bright green eyes. A quiet, friendly and affectionate tem-

perament goes with adaptability and a tendency to become one-person cats. They can be fussy feeders.

BRITISH OR AMERICAN SHORTHAIR: compact and stocky with a plush coat and big round eyes, they are the most hardy and least inbred of the pedigrees. Blue is the most popular colour, but they come in black, white, cream, tabby, tortoiseshell and bi-colours. They are gentle and affectionate with plenty of personality but are discriminating about their friends.

REX: 'pixie-shaped' faces, long legs and short curly coats. They are very lively, confident and fearless, always ready to get into mischief. As they shed no hair, they may be suitable for those who are allergic to cats.

RIGHT: *Russian blue cats are justifiably popular for the striking colour of their fur.*

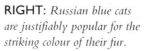

9

CAT COSTS

Over its lifetime, a cat will cost you several thousands of pounds, so it makes sense to consider the costs involved before you buy.

Take into account:

* Initial outlay: bed, litter tray, feeding bowls, carrier (see Chapter 2).
* Food: reckon on at least a can of cat food each day.
* Litter: a 'must' for every cat but if your cat is kept indoors, your litter expenses will be high.
* Neutering: more expensive for females than males.
* Vaccinations and annual boosters.
* Veterinary bills for sickness: an unknown quantity.

WHERE TO FIND YOUR PEDIGREE CAT

A pedigree cat should be obtained from a reputable breeder, preferably someone recommended by a satisfied customer. If this is not possible, contact the society devoted to your chosen breed. You can find these through cat magazines or through the organizers of local cat shows. The society will probably be able to supply a list of breeders and may even be able to tell you who has a litter available in your area. It might also be worth the effort of visiting one of the major cat shows, where you can meet breeders and their cats.

CAT COLOURS

TABBY: covers a wide range of patterns and may be striped, spotted or ticked. It is the basic coat colour of the wild cat because it provides good camouflage in the countryside.

BLACK: considered lucky in Britain, unlucky in North America, black cats have a reputation for being 'difficult'.

WHITE: the dominant white gene may be linked to deafness, particularly in blue-eyed cats. White cats have delicate skin which may need protection from too much sunlight.

TORTOISESHELL: a mixture of black, yellow and orange. Almost always female, with the few males usually sterile.

GINGER: range from cream to reddish-orange, and because the underlying pattern of the coat is tabby, they are often striped. Gingers are usually male and trainers report that they are the easiest cats to handle.

LEFT: *A kitten peeps through the bannister rails as it plays on the stairs.*

RIGHT: *A small ginger kitten poses itself prettily in front of the camera.*

WHERE TO FIND YOUR CAT

ABOVE: *It rarely takes long for a kitten to find the most comfortable place in the house.*

Friends can be the best source, because you will know the background of the litter and will have time to get to know the kittens and make your choice, as well as ensuring that your kitten has its first inoculation and leaves its mother at the right time.

A pet shop is probably the worst source. However devoted the staff may be, kittens displayed in cages or pens, with nowhere to hide and strangers tapping the netting and peering at them all day long, are under stress. This makes them more prone to illness and more vulnerable to germs passed on by other animals in a confined space.

Cat rescue groups and shelters can be a rich hunting ground: you can find their addresses from the phone book or through the local veterinarian. They usually have plenty of cats in desperate need of new homes, some of them rescued strays, others pets whose owners can no longer keep them. Kittens are often available between May and late autumn but will be in very short supply early in the year. A worker from the group will probably come and inspect your home and you will be expected to make a donation.

If a stray cat wants to make its home with you, make sure that it really is a stray before adopting it. A distraught owner may be searching high and low for it, or it may have a perfectly good home a couple of streets away and simply be hoping for a second set of meals. Once it shows serious signs of moving in, make inquiries with local veterinarians and rescue centres, put a card in the newsagent's window and perhaps a 'Found' notice in the local newspaper. It is in your own interests, because if the owner finally locates the cat in six months' or a year's time, you will have to part with it, however upsetting this may be.

PICK OF THE LITTER

When you go to choose a kitten, ask the owner to let you see the whole litter, with their mother. Even if some of the kittens are already 'booked', it makes sense to see the whole family as it is much easier to judge temperament when you see the litter-mates together. It is important to see the mother, to check that she is fit and healthy: a weak, sickly mother will mean that the kittens have a poor start in life and will probably develop health problems. This not only means large veterinary bills but a good deal of heartache too.

Before you let yourself fall for an endearing kitten, make sure that the home is clean and that the litter is regularly handled by a caring owner. Kittens born and brought up in a garage or barn, with very little human company, are unlikely to make satisfactory pets. They need to spend their first few weeks as part of the household, becoming accustomed to all the normal family activities.

Watch the kittens playing for a few minutes. When you decide which one you like, make certain that it moves freely, with no hint of a limp, and that it is alert and playful. When you pick it up gently and put it on your lap, it should be inquisitive and eager to investigate. If it spits and snarls, put it back and try another one; an aggressive kitten may well have a health problem. Most experts advise against choosing a shy, retiring kitten, even if it is particularly appealing, and this is sensible for the average household. However, for an elderly or single owner or a settled, peaceful household, willing to take a little extra trouble, a shy kitten can make a loving and affectionate pet.

BELOW: *High-spirited from the start, three kittens play together while their mother looks on.*

EXAMINING A KITTEN

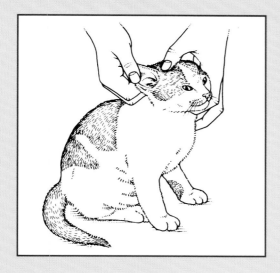

🐾 **THE COAT** should be soft, smooth and glossy, with no tangles or matting. Part the fur and look for the tiny black specs that indicate flea infestation: fleas are more likely to be found under the chin, at the base of the spine and behind the ears.

🐾 **THE BODY** should be firm, and the ribs well-covered, with a slightly rounded abdomen, but no pot-belly.

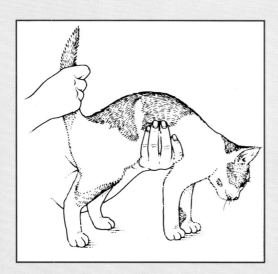

🐾 **THE EYES** should be bright and clear – definitely not runny – and there should be no third eyelids (the little triangles of tissue at the inner corners of the eyes) showing.

🐾 **THE NOSE** should be velvety, cool and slightly damp. There should be no discharge or encrustation.

🐾 **THE EARS** should be clean and the inside should look slightly moist. there should be no red-brown wax visible.

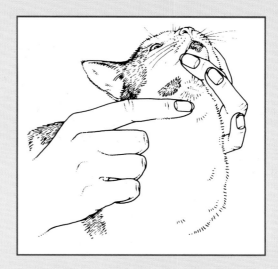

🐾 **THE ANAL AREA** should be clean, with no staining.

🐾 **THE MOUTH** should be pink and clean, with no sign of soreness or inflammation and the teeth white.

🐾 **FINALLY**, be sure to *smell* your kitten. Like a clean baby, a healthy kitten smells delightful. Any unpleasant odour indicates a problem.

Chapter 2
THE NEW ARRIVAL

Whether you are acquiring a kitten or a full-grown cat, whether it is destined to be an 'only' cat or be part of a whole feline family, there are preparations to be made. The new arrival will need its own set of equipment and, if you have other pets, it should have a short period of quarantine and some careful introductions.

BASIC EQUIPMENT

There is little point in spending money on a bed for a small kitten; it will be just as comfortable in a cardboard box, with high sides for security but a door cut in the side for easy entrance. Line the box with several layers of newspaper, then a couple of old sweaters so that it can snuggle down in the warmth – and get used to your smell at the same time. If the kitten is very nervous, invert the box and make up a soft bed underneath it, so that the kitten has a safe hidey-hole.

For older cats, pet shops offer a variety of beds. Wicker baskets look attractive and cats seem to like the creaky noise they make, but they are difficult to keep clean. Plastic beds are hygienic and functional and cosy 'igloos' with hooded tops are machine washable. Some cats love bean bags as they can knead them into shape, choosing a soft hollow in the middle on chilly nights and lying on the outer edges in warmer weather. Unfortunately, trampling on polystyrene beads seems to put some cats in mind of the litter tray, with inevitable results. Sheepskin hammocks which hang on a radiator are appreciated by the sort of cats who insist on settling in the warmest place in the house.

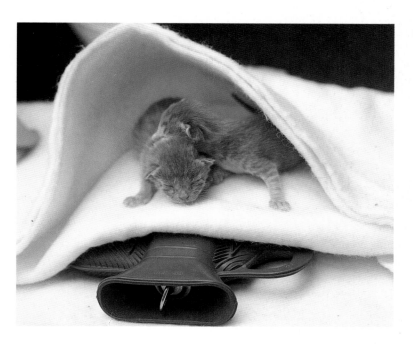

ABOVE: *Newborn kittens enjoy the warmth of a well-protected hot water bottle.*

OPPOSITE: *Endearingly playful though they are, the destructive capacity of an eight-week-old kitten should never be underestimated.*

15

ABOVE: *Cardboard boxes are often more popular than the most expensive and luxurious catbeds.*

Whichever bed you choose, it should be big enough to allow the cat to stretch out and should be placed in a quiet, draught-free spot. A heating pad will provide extra comfort when the house gets cold overnight, but place it to one side of the bed, so that the cat can chose its own temperature.

You may find that a square of carpet on top of the refrigerator or a piece of blanket on top of a high kitchen cupboard proves a more popular resting place than the most expensive bed.

Each cat must have its own feeding bowl so that they do not have to jostle for food - though they tend to change over bowls while eating, just to see if the next one contains anything better. Pottery bowls are more stable and easier to clean than plastic

ones. For hygiene, keep a special set of cutlery and can-opener for dealing with cat food and wash all cat bowls separately from family dishes. Cats like to take food out of bowls and spread it on the floor, so a wide plastic mat over the feeding area is a good idea! Plastic lids to seal opened cat-food cans are useful, as the food keeps fresher and retains more of its tempting smell.

KITTEN TIPS

★ Always keep a kitten indoors until at least a week after its second vaccination.

★ Never smack a kitten. It will not understand why you are punishing it and may learn to fear you.

★ Always allow the new kitten enough sleeping time. Keep play sessions to five or ten minutes, then give the kitten time to calm down and rest.

★ Never let a kitten (or a cat, for that matter) play with plastic bags; the risk of suffocation is too great.

★ Always accustom your kitten to gentle grooming right from the beginning, so that it accepts this as part of normal routine.

THE FIRST DAYS

A kitten should leave its mother only when it is fully weaned, at about eight weeks, and never earlier than six weeks. Breeders of pedigree cats used to keep their kittens until 12 weeks, but many now release them at 10 weeks, as they find cats settle better in their new home at that age. Plan to bring home your new pet at a time when you are not too busy to give plenty of attention to the settling-in process. If possible, arrange to collect your kitten by car, and schedule the collection for well after a mealtime. If a cat is car-sick on its first journey, it may resist car trips ever afterwards. Take details of the diet your kitten has been eating and stick to it in the early days, then make any changes very gradually.

When you get home, confine the newcomer to one room at first, providing a litter tray and a bed with a warm hot water bottle tucked under the blanket so that your kitten will not miss the warmth of its mother too much. If you have other cats, this quarantine is essential, so that no germs are passed on. Your new kitten/cat may seem perfectly healthy but it may be incubating some infectious disease that has not yet shown symptoms, particularly if it has been mixing with other cats in its previous home.

Wash and disinfect your hands each time you leave the newcomer and, if you have any doubts about its health, change your outer clothes and shoes so that you are certain you are not spreading infection.

Spend plenty of time with the new arrival, but do not let other pets feel neglected, missing their playtime or having to wait for meals, or they will begin to resent the interloper. If they show signs of gathering round the stranger's door, scratching and making hostile noises, distract them with a game.

Most kittens, so long as they are approached quietly and gently, will settle in quite quickly but a nervous kitten may hide in the most inaccessible spot it can find and refuse to eat at first. Never make the mistake of hauling a kitten out of its hidey-hole: sit down near it and talk to it soothingly. Try waggling a pencil or pulling a toy mouse on a string very slowly across the floor; the kitten may well play with you long before it will cuddle with you. Put food down at each mealtime and leave the room so that the kitten feels it can venture out in safety. Remove the bowl an hour or so later, whether the food has been eaten or not, and keep a bowl of fresh water available at all times. Let the kitten come out and approach you in its own time and respond gently to its advances, without pouncing. Follow much the same strategy with an older cat, uncertain about this new move.

RIGHT: *Two eight-week-old kittens 'embrace' during an exciting session of play fighting.*

Introductions all round

Once the new cat has settled down enough to allow itself to be petted and picked up - which may be five minutes or several days - you can begin introducing the other people in the household, one by one. Children should not be left alone with the cat and should not be allowed to pick it up at this stage. If there are no other pets, the door of its room can be left open once it has met and accepted all the family members, so that it can gradually enlarge its territory.

If you already have a resident cat, the two will by this time be accustomed to one another's smells but this does not mean they will greet each other with delight. You may have bought the newcomer for the benefit of your cat, thinking it needs a playmate and companion, but at first it will see only a usurper. For the first meeting, take your cat into the newcomer's room, then supervise but try not to interfere. Probably you will see two sets of hackles rise and two tails puff out as both cats try to make themselves look as large and menacing as possible. There may then be a stand-off as they try to stare one another out, accompanied by some blood- curdling yowling. These confrontations seldom lead to a full-scale fight but if this does happen, a cupful of cold water should break it up. A kitten pen can be useful; make sure that the newcomer and resident take turns inside.

A cat will usually accept a new kitten more easily than a full-grown cat. Once the kitten has been taught its place in the hier-

OPPOSITE: *Introduce animal members of the household gradually and under strict supervision.*

BELOW: *Simple, homemade toys will keep a young kitten happy for hours.*

18

ABOVE: *If introductions are made in a sensitive way, there is no reason why cats and dogs should not learn to live happily together.*

archy, the two will normally co-exist quite peacefully and this should take place within a few weeks. Older cats may take months and, in some cases, they learn only to tolerate one another – not an ideal situation but one not unknown in the human world.

Restrain your dog on a leash during introductions and make it quite clear that no chasing is allowed. Most cats manage to put a family dog in its place quite quickly but to begin with they should not be allowed to get too close and must never be left unsupervised until they have accepted one another completely, which may take several weeks. Some cats have become firm friends with rabbits, guinea pigs and even white mice, but don't count on it. They are much more likely to regard small animals as natural prey so it is safer to make sure that each animal has a separate living area and the cat's tolerance is never put to the test.

HANDLING A CAT

If your kitten has a calm temperament, you can hold it in the palm of your hand but, if it is a wriggler, take it gently by the scruff of the neck, with your other hand supporting its behind. You risk hurting it if you hold it by the scruff only.

Pick up your cat with one hand under its tummy and the other under its behind. You can then hold it in the crook of your arm with a hand under its front paws or you can prop it against your shoulder. Never lift it up with hands round its middle and the back half of its body dangling uncomfortably.

A cat will enjoy being handled by people if it is held comfortably and securely with two hands.

Teach children to handle the new kitten carefully by using two hands and keeping its bottom supported at all times.

LITTER MATTERS

Your kitten may come to you fully trained by its mother in the use of the litter tray, but even if it does not, there are usually few problems. Soon after a meal, a kitten will begin sniffing round for a suitable toilet area, so this is the moment to pick it up and place it in the litter tray.

If it doesn't catch on right away, scratch around in the litter with your fingers or a pencil as encouragement. When a kitten squats anywhere but in the tray with its nose in the air, it should be speedily transferred.

Keep the tray in the same place so that the kitten always knows where to find it and site it in a quiet corner, away from too many tramping feet. It should be well separated from the feeding bowls as most cats refuse to feed and toilet in the same area. A plastic seed tray is a good choice for a kitten but for a grown cat the tray should be at least 38cm (15in) square with sides about 8cm (3in) high. Some types come with a plastic ring that fastens round the top to prevent litter scattering far and wide. Others have a cover over the whole tray, with a door to allow the cat to enter, though you can make your own version far more cheaply with an upturned cardboard box of the right size to fit tightly over the tray. The privacy afforded by the cover may make all the difference to the occasional cat that seems reluctant to use a litter tray.

The most widely used cat litter is dried clay (called Fuller's earth) which absorbs both moisture and smells well, and it should be used at a depth of about 6cm (2in), to allow the cat to dig. Wood-based litters come in the form of pellets formed from sawdust and these, too, are very absorbent and have a naturally pleasant smell. A washable litter which can be used for months is used with a specially designed tray which allows urine to pass straight through to another tray below, so that it can be

ABOVE: *Cats soon become accustomed to using well-attended litter trays.*

OPPOSITE: *Giving a pill can be relatively painless for all concerned if you follow a few simple steps (see page 88).*

emptied away. This has great practical advantages, but the one slight drawback, especially for owners who are out all day, is that there is no odour-absorption for faeces. Some owners use layers of shredded newspaper in the litter tray but you need to be a household of heavy readers, not to mention good shredders, as they will need to be changed frequently.

Most cats will only use a clean tray but this does not mean that you have to change the entire litter every day, or even every week, unless your cat is extra fussy. Simply scoop out wet litter and solid waste at least twice a day and refill with new litter. You will soon get to know your cat's preference: some prefer their tray to smell 'catty', others refuse to use it a second time until it has been cleaned. Stand the tray on a piece of vinyl, which can be taken up and cleaned when necessary.

REGULAR VETERINARY CARE

Every kitten should be vaccinated against feline infectious enteritis and feline respiratory disease (cat flu), both viruses which can cause serious illness and even death. The kitten has

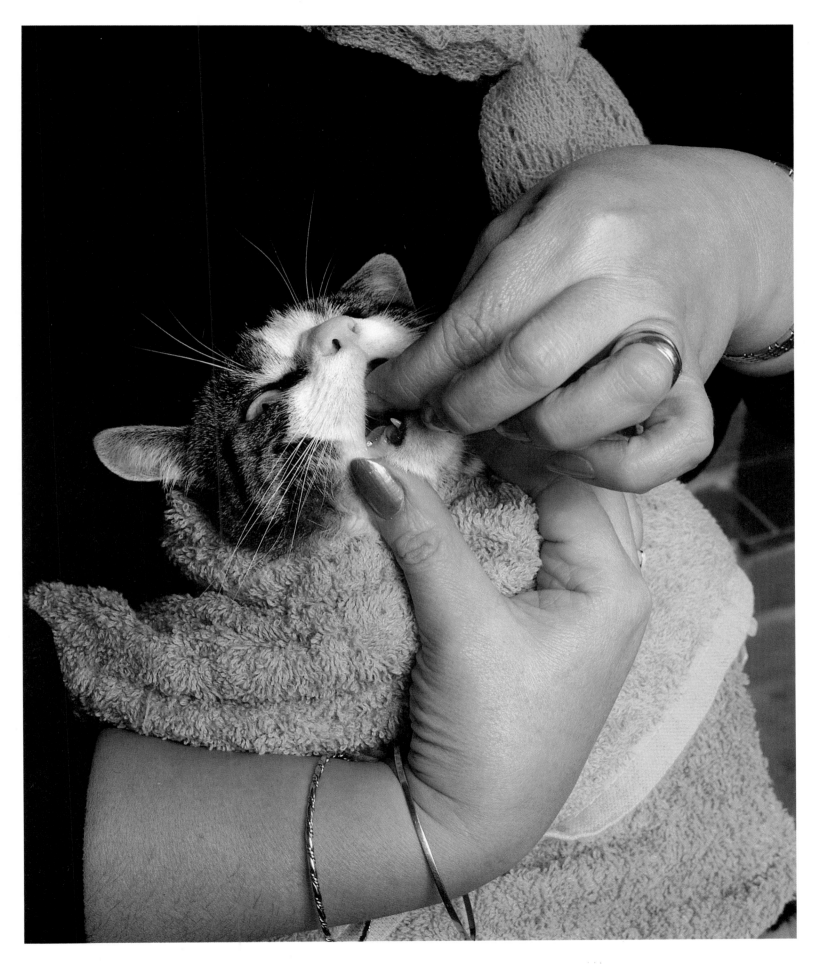

some immunity from its mother's milk for the first few weeks of its life, but needs its first injection at about ten weeks and the second three or four weeks later. After that it will need an annual booster. A previous owner who tells you that a cat has already been vaccinated must be able to provide proof in the form of a signed veterinary certificate. Most catteries will not accept a cat without such proof.

There is now a vaccination available against feline leukaemia, a fatal and incurable disease which destroys the cat's immune system, making it vulnerable to all sorts of infections. This requires

a blood test (to make sure that the cat is not already infected) followed by a first injection, then a second two or three weeks later, and an annual booster.

Cats should also be treated regularly against roundworms and tapeworms and at your first visit your veterinarian will advise on suitable preparations and when they should be given.

NEUTER OR NOT?

Most owners will want their cats neutered unless they are planning to use them for breeding purposes. Without the operation tom-cats become very smelly as they spray their territory (indoors as well as outdoors) and get into frequent fights which can leave them with painful abscesses. An un-neutered female will regularly come into oestrus or 'season' and if allowed out, she will produce litter after litter - and it may be extremely dif-

BELOW: *A visit to the veterinarian for an ophthalmic examination.*

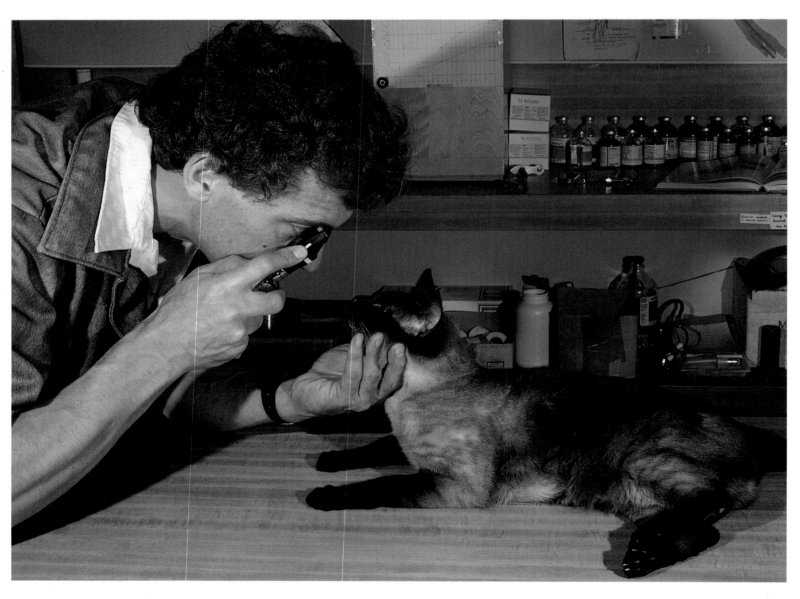

ABOVE: *New kittens lose no time in seeking out the most dare-devil games in the garden.*

ficult to find homes for the kittens. If you keep her indoors she will wear herself out with fruitless 'calling' and if she keeps coming into season without producing a litter, she may develop an ovarian cyst. Your veterinarian will advise on the right age for neutering your cat. For most females this will be around five

months, as they may begin calling at seven months and sometimes even earlier. At one time there was a theory that a female should be allowed to produce one litter before being spayed but there is no good reason for this. Some owners only spay after the first litter so that they can keep one of the kittens, but this does not usually work out well. Female cats seem to regard it as unnatural if their kittens do not leave home once they are weaned, and will get on much better with a strange kitten than with their own offspring.

Castrating a male is very simple and will not normally require stitches. Neutering a female involves removing the ovaries and

uterus and this requires a small incision and stitches which must be removed a week or 10 days later. The risk of the general anaesthetic to a young, healthy cat is minimal – probably less than the risks incurred by pregnancy. Both sexes can usually return home the same day and the after-effects are minimal, though the cat will usually be sleepy for the rest of the day. After that, the majority are back to normal, though sometimes a cat will remain sleepy for several days and you should keep a careful eye on it to see that it does not develop other problems. Females with stitches should be kept apart from other pets except when supervised, so make arrangements for this in advance.

OPPOSITE: *As your new kitten grows more confident, it will tentatively start to explore its new home.*

BELOW: *Hand-rearing a kitten with a proprietary feeding bottle filled with a cat milk replacement product.*

THE GREAT OUTDOORS

When it is time for your new kitten or cat to venture outside:

* ★ Give it plenty of fuss before you open the door.

* ★ Choose a time shortly before a meal is due, so that the cat will come in when it hears its food being prepared.

* ★ Accompany your cat on its first jaunts; it may have arrived in the middle of another's cat's territory.

* ★ Never let your cat out at night.

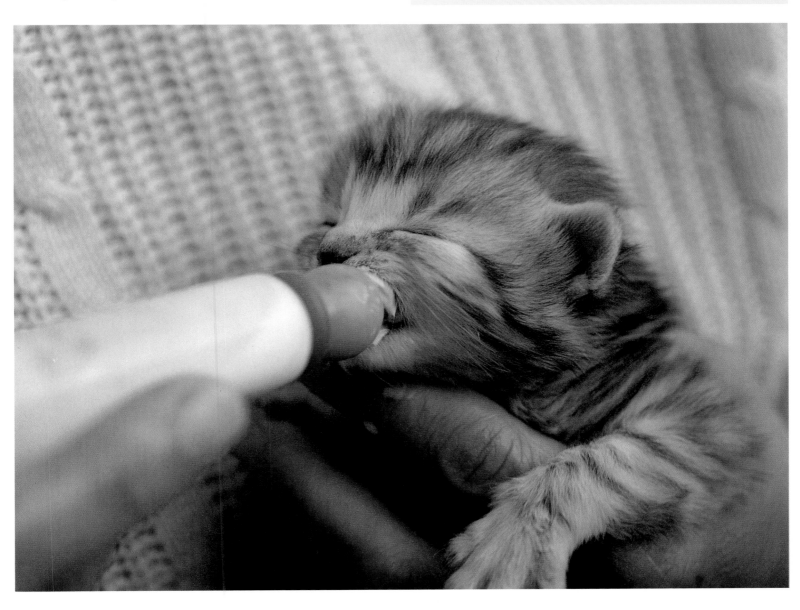

If you adopt an adult cat without knowing its background, it is easy enough to tell if a male has been neutered, but it may be impossible to tell if a female has been spayed, unless the veterinarian can locate the tiny surgical scar. He may have to operate to discover if the uterus is intact and then remove it if this proves necessary.

SPECIAL CASES

Hand-rearing a kitten

Sometimes new arrivals can be especially taxing: a cat-lover may have found a litter of helpless, abandoned kittens in the garden, or perhaps your own cat gives birth and is unable to feed the kittens. There are four basic choices: ask the veterinarian to put them to sleep, find a cat rescue charity willing to take them, find a cat that might foster them – or rear them by hand. Hand-rearing is a demanding job, so think hard before you undertake it. The kittens will have to be kept very warm – at 27°-30°C (81°-86°F) for the first fortnight, then cooling gradually to about 21°C (70°F) at six weeks – and they will need feeding at all hours of the day and night.

The kittens should be fed with a proper kitten feeding bottle, available from pet shops, and these must be sterilized after every use. Use a special cat milk replacement product, made up according to the instructions on the packet. After feeding, you will need to wipe the anal area with cotton wool moistened with warm water. This replaces the mother's licking action to stimulate urination and defecation.

From three weeks you can gradually begin weaning the kittens by adding a little finely puréed fish or meat babyfood to the milk meals, which will be offered at slightly increasing intervals and amounts until, at four weeks, four times a day is sufficient. At five weeks substitute a feed of very finely minced white meat or puréed poached white fish for one of the milk meals. Two meat or fish meals and two milk meals will suffice at five weeks, and after that the amount of solid food can be increased with a good quality canned kitten food being introduced which will replace the milk feeds over the next fortnight. By eight weeks the kittens will usually be fully weaned and ready to go to new homes. Their owners will be very fortunate, for hand-reared kittens are especially affectionate.

The stray arrival

Before taking in a well-fed 'stray', heed the warnings given in Chapter 1. However, there may be a time when you take pity on a thin, unkempt cat that has been wandering the neighbourhood for weeks and think of giving it a permanent home. If you have cats already, think twice. Strays may be carrying dangerous infections and it might be safer to ask for help from a cat rescue charity, who can often make arrangements to trap and care for a sad stray. Often such cats are unneutered toms, bearing the scars of many a battle, or pregnant females (recognizable by their bulging tummies) and they have been turned out by owners who did not bother to have them neutered and now find them too much trouble to care for. Cats that have had a hard life will be very timid, and to begin with, you should be content to leave food in a quiet spot outdoors. Once the cat is taking food regularly you can retreat less and less from the feeding spot and once it is willing to eat while you sit close by, it has probably accepted you and you can begin to initiate a friendship. Don't be tempted to overfeed a hungry stray or you could cause a bad upset in its digestive system.

It may take months before the cat is prepared to come indoors but you can then make arrangements for veterinary inspection and neutering if necessary. Unless it is very young and the veterinarian can tell its age from its teeth – if it still has its milk teeth it is under seven months old – you will probably never know the age of your stray cat, though the veterinarian may make a guess from its general condition.

NEW-BORN KITTEN FEEDS

AGE	AMOUNT	WHEN TO FEED
Up to 7 days	3-5ml (½-1 teaspoon)	2 hourly
7-14 days	5-7ml (1-1½ teaspoons)	2 hourly during day, 4 hourly at night
14-21 days	7-10ml (1½-2 teaspoons)	2 hourly during day with a 6-hour break from midnight

OPPOSITE: *Think twice before adopting strays, particularly if you have cats already, as they can harbour dangerous infections. If you feel that a local stray needs care and attention, one solution is to contact a cat rescue charity.*

Chapter 3
FOOD AND FEEDING

Cats are selective about what they eat and will usually inspect any meal offered very carefully before taking a mouthful. Smell and temperature are as important to them as taste, and their highly developed senses enable them to detect any slight loss of freshness not apparent to their owners.

They like variety in their diet and can become bored with the same food day after day, but their reputation as fussy eaters is much exaggerated. When an owner reports that a cat will only eat smoked salmon and prawns or poached breast of chicken, it is usually because cats are very good at manipulating their owners. They are quite capable of sitting beside their untouched breakfast mewing hungrily for an hour, if they know that in the end something delicious will be provided.

KITTEN CARE

Kittens have small stomachs, so they need feeding several times a day. From two to four months of age they should have four meat meals a day. There are proprietary brands of food specially formulated for kittens and, as a general rule, 200-300g (7-10oz) a day should be sufficient, but be guided by your kitten's appetite and don't worry if its sides bulge after a good meal. You can provide variety by occasionally adding a little fresh meat or fish or cooked vegetables like carrot, cabbage or potato, finely chopped. The meat or fish should be cooked and never served raw. At four months, reduce the number of meals to three, but feed a larger quantity each time, and at six months,

FEEDING DO'S AND DON'TS

* **Do** feed your cat at a regular time and always in the same place.

* **Don't** serve food intended for dogs; it will not contain all the nutrients your cat needs.

* **Do** serve all meals at room temperature, not straight from the refrigerator.

* **Don't** feed your cat snacks between meals.

* **Do** cook fish, poultry and pork; never serve them raw.

move to the adult feeding pattern of two meals a day. Establish a disciplined approach to eating by always serving food in the same place at the same time and by avoiding the pitfall of snacks between meals.

OPPOSITE: *A tabby and white tortoiseshell is curious to know what her owner has selected for her supper.*

THE ADULT DIET

ABOVE: *A young ginger cat steals away after enjoying scraps from under the table.*

Most owners find that the most convenient way of feeding a balanced diet is to use canned cat food as the staple food. Providing that the label states that it is a 'complete' food, you can be sure that it will cater for all the nutritional requirements of a healthy cat. When you are choosing a brand, pick one that contains around 8% protein and little or no cereal. All sorts of flavours are offered and your cat will have its own favourite, but the basic contents will vary very little: the main ingredients will be slaughterhouse waste products unfit for human consumption and waste products from the fish canning industry. Added flavouring and odours make the difference in taste, so you don't need to choose one particular type because it is more nutritious.

Appetites vary, but an average amount of food would be eight heaped tablespoons a day. The 'gourmet' brands contain a much larger proportion of meat, so less will be needed. If the cat's basic diet was fatty meat, oily fish or chicken, the amount needed could be cut by half, but feeding a cat entirely on home-cooked food is a tricky business, and you would need to use various supplements: sterilized bonemeal, meat or yeast extract, cod liver oil and so on, all in the correct proportions. It is easier, and more sensible, to provide variety in the diet by giving your cat fresh food two or three times a week.

The 'variety' meals might be beef, lamb or pork - with a sprinkling of carrots, green vegetables, or a little pasta - tinned sar-

32

dines, tuna or mackerel, diced chicken with the skin left on, or white fish with a little cooked rice. Boiling fish destroys the nutrients, so poach it gently instead and remove all bones before serving. When serving meat, remember that cats cannot chew like humans, so pieces should either be bite-sized, or large enough to allow the cat to tear at them. Liver – very popular with many cats – should not be given more than once a week as it is very high in vitamin A and this can cause bowel problems.

Dried food can be extremely useful as it can be stored for longer and left down by owners who have to be away from home most of the day. The problem is that it contains only about 10% water, as compared with 75% or more in canned food, and cats need to drink more water if they are on this type of diet. If they don't, urinary problems may result. It may be wiser to give a little dried food as an extra treat along with the normal diet. It is good for the cat's teeth, helping to prevent tartar build-up, and most cats seem to love the taste. Alternatively, veterinarians sell a dried food that has been formulated to avoid health problems.

THE CARNIVOROUS CAT

Some vegetarian owners have tried to extend their principles to their pets, but cats are essentially carnivores and need meat to survive. Though they can digest some vegetable matter, their bodies cannot manufacture some of the essential amino-acids not provided by a vegetarian diet. Any owners who cannot bear to see an animal devouring meat should find another home for their cats.

BELOW: *Provide each of your cats with their own feeding bowl and encourage them to develop a regular eating place.*

GRASS-EATING

Cats love chewing grass and it is very useful as an emetic, helping the cat to vomit and get rid of furballs and other unwanted matter. It also provides the cat with extra vitamins, such as folic acid. If your cat chews happily at the edge of the lawn, make sure that you do not use fertilizers or herbicides that would be harmful to pets. For an indoor cat you can provide specially grown grass, available in tubs from pet shops. If your cat seems to need to eat grass morning, noon and night, it may be indicative of a gut infection, so check with your veterinarian.

While grass chewing is quite a common habit,
nibbling at flowers is probably simply playfulness.

DRINKING

ABOVE: *Some cats prefer to drink water from the fish pond where the smells are more interesting than those found in a saucer of tapwater.*

Cats are essentially desert animals and can survive for a surprisingly long time without water. Under normal domestic circumstances, they absorb most of the fluid they need from their food and may seem to drink very little. However, your cat should always have access to fresh water which has not been standing all day to acquire a layer of dust, even if you never see it drinking. Don't use a tiny bowl, as cats like to drink from containers that are at least as wide as their whiskers.

There is nothing unusual about a cat preferring to drink from the birdbath, the fishpond or even a puddle – it seems that they offer more interesting smells than chemically treated tapwater. Some cats dislike the smell of freshly drawn tapwater and will only drink after it has been standing for a while; others only like to drink from a running tap, perhaps because of some 'race memory' that tells them running water is safer than standing pools. Occasionally a cat will decide that the toilet offers the most palatable supply of water but this should be discouraged by keeping the toilet lid closed.

Contrary to widespread belief, milk is not necessary to a cat's diet. Though cow's milk contains valuable nutrients, many cats cannot digest it and it gives them diarrhoea.

OPPOSITE: *A saucer of milk on a summer's day is much appreciated.*

a few meals and it will not allow itself to starve. Once it gets used to the new menu, cut down the amount of the special delicacy bit by bit.

FAT CATS

Most cats regulate their calorie intake well and will walk away from a plate of food when they have had enough, but some are just plain greedy. Your cat is overweight if its sides bulge when viewed head on, or if you cannot feel its ribs by gentle pressure. Though obesity does not have the disastrous effect on cats that it has on dogs and humans, it does put an extra strain on the heart, liver and kidneys and so is better avoided.

FUSSY FEEDERS

Fussy cats usually have over-indulgent owners, willing to cater for every whim: if the cat does not gobble up the food provided with obvious relish, they fear that it will suffer dire effects and hasten to provide something more tempting. It does not take long for a habit to form, and then the cat has you just where it wants.

There may be some good reason why your cat picks at its food instead of eating properly: perhaps its food bowl is in a busy area, where it is disturbed by children or dogs, or it has a small appetite and would prefer several small meals, rather than two substantial ones. When a cat paws the ground around its food, many owners assume that it is rejecting the food and asking for something different. In fact, all it means is that the cat is not hungry enough to eat the food at the moment: in the wild it would have to cover up the food to protect it from other animals, and would return to it later. Allow your cat to do the same at home, rather than hastening to produce an alternative.

If you have already fallen for your cat's ploys and find that it now refuses everything but some special delicacy, you are doing it no favours, as it will not be getting a balanced diet. Try putting things right by chopping the favourite food very finely and mixing it with a similarly flavoured canned catfood. If your cat refuses to eat it, leave it down for a reasonable length of time, then remove it. Ignore all the 'starving cat' pleas and serve an identical meal next time. It will do your cat no harm to miss

You may be able to slim your not-too-overweight cat by providing a diet lower in fat for a few weeks: serve the 'gourmet' range of canned food, fish or rabbit and give several small meals instead of two large ones, cutting down the overall amount. Cut out milk and dried food and add a pinch of bran to the cat's meal for extra fibre. If your cat is already obese, consult your veterinarian: he may suggest a prescription, low-calorie diet. Unfortunately, unless your cat lives indoors it may well go 'shopping' round the neighbourhood for extra food, even snatching it from the plates of other cats. If you have cat-loving neighbours who find it hard to resist, explain what you are trying to do and ask them to co-operate.

ELDERLY CATS

The average lifespan of a domestic cat is 12-15 years, which would equate with 65-75 in humans, and a 20-year-old cat can be regarded as a centenarian. As your cat grows older, its appetite may change and it may need smaller and more frequent meals. It now needs less protein but what it has must be high quality and it will be able to digest chicken, rabbit and fish bet-ter than red meat. As it loses weight and may be suffering from kidney problems, you should add extra carbohydrates in the form of bread, finely chopped potato or pasta and rice cooked in tasty stock to the food.

Constipation will be helped by serving only fish with a pinch of bran. A teaspoon of lard mixed in with meals will supply extra calories. Encourage your cat to drink by serving warm water and milk.

If an elderly cat eats very slowly, it may be that its mouth is hurting and your veterinarian will be able to advise on any treatment needed. In any case an old cat should have regular veterinary checkups and your veterinarian may recommend a vitamin supplement or even a special prescription diet.

BELOW: *Most cats take ageing in their stride but it is worth taking extra care with their diet to maintain good health.*

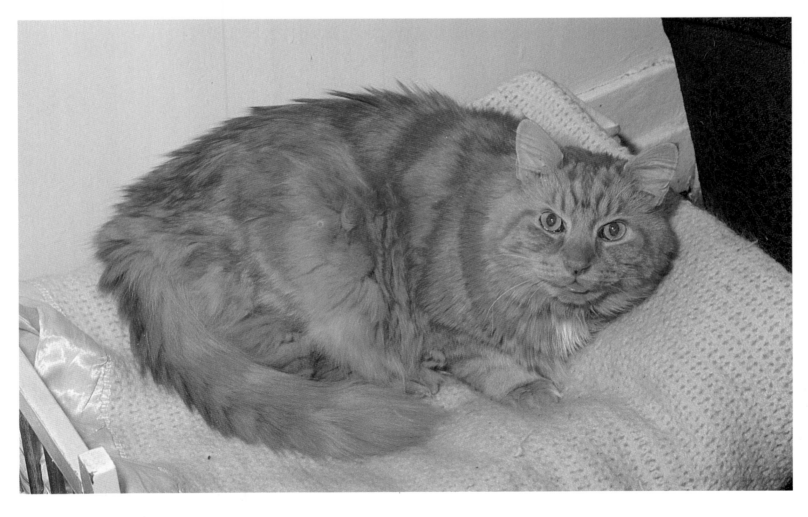

Chapter 4
UNDERSTANDING YOUR CAT

Cats have a popular reputation as aloof and independent, but most owners find that they develop

a close understanding with their feline pets. The more you talk to your cat, the more it comes to

recognize and respond to your tone of voice – and the same is true the other way round.

CAT TALK

Most domestic cats develop a range of miaows to signify their wants, because they find they work well: the 'I'm hungry' miaow will be quite different from the 'let me out' miaow or the 'cuddle me' miaow. Besides miaowing, they may have a vocabulary ranging from the teeth-clicking sounds of high excitement when watching a bird on the window-ledge, to a blood-curdling howl intended to scare away next door's trespassing tom.

Purring is usually associated with contentment and relaxation and there's nothing more relaxing than having a purring cat on your lap. As a general rule, the happier the cat, the rougher and louder the purr; some cats get so carried away that they end up coughing and spluttering. As the cat becomes sleepy and pre-

ABOVE: *A cat's body is very expressive and it uses its eyes, ears and even whiskers to show its feelings.*

OPPOSITE: *The arched back, flattened ears and 'bottlebrush' tail are all signs of the kitten's determination to scare off an intruder - never mind its size*

ABOVE: *A cat's eyes give the clearest indication of its mood. This tabby and white cat contracts its eyes as it begins to relax.*

pares to settle down, the purr becomes softer and gentler, subsiding into a faint buzz. Scientists have never been able to agree on an explanation for the purring mechanism, which does not come simply from the larynx but from deep within the cat's body. One theory is that it is caused by the vibration of the blood supply passing through a large vein in the cat's chest; another is that it is caused by changes of air pressure causing vibration within the respiratory system. Whatever the explana-

tion, the purr vibration can be felt through the cat's throat and ribs. Purring is not always associated with happiness: a cat may purr when it is frightened - for instance when it is taken to the veterinarian or left in a cattery for the first time. This may be a way of comforting itself or simply a signal to the rest of the world that it is inoffensive and non-threatening.

BODY LANGUAGE

The cat's body is very expressive, as it uses its eyes, ears, tail, posture and even its whiskers to show its feelings. There is no mistaking the message when two cats confront one another angrily: an angry cat determined to scare off an intruder will arch its body, the fur bristling along its spine and the erect tail fluffed out like a brush. It moves sideways on stiff legs, its ears flattened back against its head, its pupils wide and its mouth open to show its teeth, giving out a fearsome growl or yowl. When a cat is on the defensive it may hunch its body or even cringe in submission, its whiskers and ears flattened, its gaze intense to catch any movement from the aggressor, its tail thumping the ground.

The tail is a dependable barometer of a cat's mood. An upright tail means that the cat is friendly and confident and a bend at the tip signifies real pleasure or happiness. If the tail is horizontal, the cat is unsure and a dragging tail means that the cat is unhappy or unwell. A slowly wagging tail can signify mere

alertness, anticipation or indecision and a tail which thumps the ground repeatedly shows anger.

Every owner knows that a cat's pupils dilate widely in response to anger, fright or excitement, then contract to tiny slits when the cat is relaxed and pleased with life. Rapid blinking shows anxiety but a long, slow blink is a sign of trust, friendship and contentment.

THE FLEHMAN RESPONSE

Owners are often puzzled when they see their cat open its mouth slightly and draw back its lips in a grimace, something like a silent growl. This is called the 'Flehman response' and carries no message to humans; the cat is using its unique ability to test out the environment by drawing air across a special organ in the roof of its mouth which enables it to taste and smell at the same time. This response is far more noticeable in the big cats – lions and tigers – than in their domestic relatives, but you may see your cat using it to test the readiness of a female for mating, or if it senses danger.

BELOW: *A ginger male flattens his ears and shows his teeth to deter an unwelcome visitor.*

When the cat is alert and pleased with life, its ears are pricked up and facing straight ahead; if it becomes annoyed, the ears pull back towards the side. Twitching ears may indicate that the cat is nervous and you may see it licking its lips as anxiety increases. When it is stalking a bird and anticipating a successful pounce, its ears sometimes flatten sideways and this gives a clear 'do not disturb' signal.

MEETING AND GREETING

When two friendly cats meet, they first sniff one another's mouths and noses, then perhaps rub along the length of their bodies and sniff one another's anal area. By this time they have collected all the information they need. If, on greeting you for the first time, a cat sniffs your face, it is offering a friendly feline 'hello' and the friendliest response you can give in return is to sniff back. Gathering it up in your arms at this point may be too forward and prevent a relationship of trust building up. You might well prefer to decline if the cat presents its rear end for the anal sniff, but a gentle stroke from the rear of the spine along the tail will do just as well as a friendly gesture. The most unfriendly thing you could do would be to make any hissing sound, which is always interpreted as a threat. This is why most cats hate the noise of aerosols or fizzy drinks cans being opened. Some experts believe that this is why cats hate being laughed at, because the sound of a laugh resembles that of a hiss - but this may well be simply because laughter is not a response that animals recognize and the cat feels excluded and resentful.

When two cats square up to one another, the hostile display always includes a great deal of staring, and if one cat can out-stare the other, it can hold its ground as the winner, so it is not surprising that cats are unnerved or frightened by staring strangers. This explains why a cat, entering a room where several cat-lovers are trying to win its attention, will unerringly pick the one cat-hater and leap straight onto that person's unwilling lap. The cat-hater has been looking the other way, so

BELOW: *Two kittens smell each other to gather the information that they need on meeting for the first time.*

ABOVE: *A cat greets a human in much the same way that it greets another cat, that is by slowly advancing and then sniffing the face in a friendly, feline 'hello'.*

the cat feels reassured and secure, blithely unaware that its attentions are unwelcome.

Of course, some cats are so confident that they will march up to you and start making overtures whatever you do, and even pushing them away will not discourage them, but if you are try-

ing to make friends with a hesitant or nervous cat, avoid looking at it directly. Sit quietly, perhaps moving a pencil or scrunching a bit of paper occasionally to interest the cat, so that it forgets its nerves. If necessary, get down to the cat's level: lie on the floor with your eyes half closed and the cat will soon come to inspect this non-threatening new person. When it does, stay quiet without reaching out and let the cat complete its investigations. When it shows acceptance by rubbing against you, then is the time to offer a gentle stroke.

Many owners find that their cats know their footsteps or the sound of their car and will run to meet them when they return home, often taking up a favourite position on a table or chair, to bring them nearer to human level for a fulsome greeting. The cat will rub its face and its body round any bit of you within reach, partly as a greeting, but partly to reinforce its ownership. Cats have scent glands around their lips and on either side of the forehead and they use them to mark the members of the family. When you have been out of the house for a while, their scent has faded and they need to renew it.

AFFECTION

One school of thought maintains that cats are far too self-serving to be capable of affection, but most cat-owners would disagree. It is true that you will only get back from the relationship what you put into it - a dog may give unswerving love and devotion to an indifferent owner but a cat will not. If you are too busy to pay it proper attention, it will make its own independent life and only demonstrate 'cupboard love' at mealtimes. However, a petted cat will show its affection very clearly. Many a cat, finding itself displaced in the family pecking order by the arrival of children, dogs, or extra cats, will feel so deprived that it seeks affection elsewhere, making a part-time home with the old lady down the street, where a welcoming lap is always on offer and the pace is somewhat slower.

A cat settling down on your lap will paddle rhythmically with its paws, wearing an expression of utter bliss. This kneading movement - which can become very uncomfortable unless you trim your cat's claws - is a throw-back to kittenhood, when your cat kneaded its mother's teats to stimulate the production of milk. It may be that it simply associates this movement with feelings of extreme pleasure, or it may be a way of telling you that in your closest moments, it thinks of you as a substitute mother. Once settled, the cat may well give your hand a thorough licking. Some experts say that they are only tasting the salt on your skin, but two friendly cats cuddling down together will often lick one another, just as their mother once licked them, and it is far more likely that this, too, is an activity associated with comfort and happiness.

RIGHT: *When its underside is exposed a cat is at its most vulnerable; a touch will either bring into play an almost automatic defence reflex or else acceptance of the caress, which indicates a very close relationship.*

When a cat rolls over onto its back with paws in the air, it looks just like an invitation to rub its tummy, but this is not necessarily the case. You may find that, in mid-rub, the cat closes on your hand and you can even get scratched or bitten. When its tummy is exposed a cat is at its most vulnerable and a touch can bring into play an almost automatic defence reflex. If a cat does let you rub its tummy while in this position, it is the sign of a very close relationship.

OPPOSITE: *The territorial instinct is as strong in urban cats, whose 'patch' may be quite small, as it is in farm cats, whose territory may be many acres.*

ABOVE: *Within the territory that it controls, a cat generally has a favourite spot for sunning itself and sleeping.*

TERRITORY

Each cat has its own territory, though the size of that territory will vary enormously. A farm cat may have a territory extending over hundreds of hectares (acres) while an urban cat may only control a few metres (yards) of backyard. The territorial instinct is very important for cats in the wild as the size of the territory dictates the size of the food supply; every poacher threatens their very existence so they fight to defend their patch against all comers. Even a cat living entirely indoors does not lose its territorial instincts and if another cat wanders too near the window it may pound on the glass, yowling in fury, then run round the edge of the room, redefining the territory and making sure that the interloper has not managed to creep in by another route.

When a number of cats live in the same neighbourhood, an unneutered tom will have the biggest territory, followed by neutered males, with females controlling the smallest area. Several cats sharing a home will usually hold their territory in common and defend it against outsiders, though one cat make stake a claim to a particular place and drive off other members

of the household. Within the territory a cat will have its favourite spots for sleeping and sunning itself, and probably a carefully selected vantage point for surveying the scene. The cat will patrol the territory regularly, probably taking exactly the same route every time, marking the boundaries with its scent by spraying, rubbing up against walls and fences and scratching trees. The scent must be renewed frequently: it will tell other cats that the territory is guarded and how recently its owner has paid a visit.

Where the properties of various cats meet, there are pathways used by several cats and there will be acknowledged areas where a number of cats will meet as part of their normal social life. When a cat strays onto territory currently held by another it does so with care. When there is a confrontation, it is usually

settled by a lot of hard staring and menacing displays, but when all else fails and there is a fight, it can be bitter and damaging. A new cat on the block often has to battle to assert claims to its own garden, which has previously formed part of another cat's territory.

HUNTING

Cats are very efficient predators and though, when they are well fed, the necessity to hunt and kill is no longer there, the instinct is still strong. The cat has two essential tools for the successful hunter: keen eyesight and acute hearing. The shape of its outer ear concentrates sound and it can move its ears forwards and sideways to catch the slightest sound made by its prey. The field of vision of each eye overlaps by over 40, so that it can judge distance with deadly accuracy.

When pursuing its prey a cat will first approach slowly and stealthily, then it will break into a crouching run, its body close to the ground, pausing then running forward again until it is close enough to take cover for the final pounce. It then stops, its eyes unwaveringly fixed on its quarry, its tail twitching in anticipation and its haunches moving to gather momentum. Finally it launches itself forward, leaps, and pins down the prey with its front paws.

Many people are upset by the apparent cruelty of the cat as it hooks its hapless prey in its claws and tosses it in the air, or lets it go for a few seconds, only to pounce again as soon as it moves. None of this behaviour has anything to do with cruelty. The cat is not playing a game when it tosses a mouse or bird in the air; it is stunning the prey so that it will be unable to escape. However, once it has the prey pinned down, it tends to lose interest – after all, it is not hungry, so it does not need an immediate kill. Movement, however, immediately triggers its hunting instinct and it becomes excited again. If you want to rescue a bird from your cat's clutches, your best hope is to choose a moment when the bird is 'playing dead' and distract the cat with its favourite chasing game, pulling a dressing-gown cord, a piece of string with a ball attached, or a waggling pencil.

BELOW: *A wooden post has been chosen as the best vantage point for detecting intruders and surveying the scene.*

When your cat brings in some dead or mangled creature and lays it proudly at your feet, or even deposits it lovingly in your favourite armchair, it may be saying simply 'look what a clever cat I am' or it may feel that it is contributing to the family food store. Whatever its thoughts, no cries of horror or outrage from you, instead of the praise it might have been expecting, will

STALKING AND HUNTING

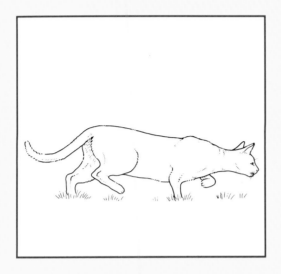

1 When pursuing its prey, the cat advances slowly with its body close to the ground.

2 The cat runs forward then pauses, then runs a little further and pauses again until it gets close to its quarry.

3 Next the cat stops still with its eyes fixed unswervingly on its victim.

4 The cat launches itself forward and traps the bird with its front paws.

give the slightest discouragement and some experts have suggested that the cat is actually trying to teach its owners how to hunt for themselves. A mother cat in the wild will first bring home dead prey so that its kittens can practise pouncing, then later live prey so that they can perfect their hunting skills with a moving target. Perhaps, after all, we are a sad disappointment to our cats.

Unfortunately, cats cannot distinguish between the house mice they are required to catch and the pretty garden birds that you would prefer them to leave alone, and it would be unkind and unfair to punish them for making the 'wrong' choice. Some owners attach bells to their cats' collars in the hope that this will warn off birds in time but the cats' stalking procedure is so stealthy that bells are of little practical value. It is much wiser not to encourage birds to come into your garden, because even if you put the feeding table well out of your cat's reach, the birds will perch on branches and fences around the garden and present a tempting prospect to the cat.

SLEEPING AND DREAMING

The cat family is not designed for continuous activity; like their wild cousins, domestic cats indulge in short bursts of activity in between long periods of rest. An adult cat sleeps about 16 hours a day - longer if there is no one at home and nothing to rouse its interest. It may well choose prime locations, such as your favourite armchair or your bed, but it may prefer a seemingly inhospitable, but warm, place like the top of the washing machine or video recorder. (For safety, always check inside your washing machine and tumble drier before switching on.) Outside, it will usually choose a high place, well out of possible

danger, and may even settle down for a quiet snooze while balanced on a narrow fence-top.

More than two-thirds of the 16 hours is spent in 'napping' and the rest is deep sleep, but even when deeply asleep, electroencephalogram (EEG) readings have shown that a cat's brain waves retain much the same pattern as during waking times, which probably explains its ability to spring up in an instant, fully awake and ready to tackle any danger. During deep sleep, cats dream about 60% of the time; this is evidenced by the Rapid Eye Movement (REM) also experienced in humans, when the eyes move beneath the closed eyelids. Presumably a cat's dreams mirror its waking experiences - the thrill and excitement of the chase, the fear of being chased, and so on - and you may see twitching legs and ears and hear little mews of excitement or distress. If the dream is obviously turning into a nightmare, you can help the cat in the same way as a human partner having a bad dream: wake it with a gentle touch and soothing words.

AGILITY

BELOW: *Spurning softer comforts, this cat has selected a cardboard box for a well-earned spell of rest and relaxation.*

Cats have the reputation for always landing on their feet, and though this does not necessarily work with a fall from a great height (cats have been hurt falling from window-ledges and balconies), cats are certainly the acrobats of the animal world. When your cat walks unwaveringly along the top of the fence, it uses its tail to regulate balance - when it turns its head one way, watch how the tail automatically moves the other way.

The unique agility of the cat is most obvious in the 'self-righting reflex' which comes into play the instant it feels itself falling.

A complex organ in the cat's inner ear, called the vestibular apparatus, tells its brain its exact position in space. An automatic sequence of movement follows, with the cat first adjusting its head and then its body into the right position for a safe landing.

SELF-RIGHTING REFLEX

1 Falling with tummy uppermost

2 The cat starts to twist

3 The cat completes the twist and rights itself

4 Ready to land with feet in position

Chapter 5
CARING FOR
YOUR CAT

Cats cost little in cash or effort compared to the pleasure they give their owners, but it is not sufficient to feed them and leave them to their own devices. A little time spent catering to your cat's needs will pay dividends in producing a lively pet in peak condition.

PLAY

Play is just as important for kittens as for children, as part of the learning process, teaching them how to cope with the world around them. When they stalk and pounce on their mother's waving tail they are beginning to practise their hunting skills, and when they ambush their litter-mates, rolling over and over in mock combat, they are learning self-defence. When a kitten jumps on another's back and seizes it by the scruff of the neck, it is rehearsing later mating behaviour - or, perhaps, the killing bite it will one day inflict on captured prey.

For cats in the wild, this play behaviour disappears when they are caught up in the adult concerns of catching food and surviving but house-cats, without the need to conserve their energy for finding the next meal, will keep a kitten's love of fun and games throughout their lives, so long as it is encouraged by their owners. Playfulness and 'larking around' gives non-hunting cats necessary exercise and strengthens the bond of affection between you and your pet. It may also discourage them from 'ambushing' your ankles or pouncing on your feet under the bedclothes.

Set aside regular times of the day for play: for kittens, five minutes at a time is sufficient, but for adults it can be anything from ten minutes to half an hour. Always build up gently and wind down the end of the play session so that the cat is not left in an excited state.

SCRATCHING POSTS

Scratching posts are also essential for a cat's well-being: a good stretch and scratch tones up the muscles and keeps the claws in trim by stripping off the outer layers and sharpening them up. The blissful look on your cat's face as it claws stretch and pull shows you how deeply ingrained, and how necessary, the

OPPOSITE: *A bright-eyed kitten in the peak of health will stay playful and 'kittenish' provided this aspect of its character is encouraged.*

scratching behaviour is. Out of doors, cats will usually find their own scratching places but a good, solid log with bark intact will be appreciated. Inside, a scratching post is essential, otherwise your upholstery will soon be hanging in ribbons. There are plenty of commercially made posts available, some basic in design, others quite expensive pieces of furniture incorporating platforms, shelves, and toys to entertain the cat. Some of the posts sold in pet-shops are far too small; they should be at least 75cm (30in) high so that the cat can reach its full height. Some manufacturers make posts that stretch from floor to ceiling. It is easy to make your own scratcher by gluing an off-cut of high quality carpet to a flat piece of wood, which is then fixed to the wall in a concealed corner, or even by wrapping sisal rope closely round a table leg. The rope or carpet can then be replaced as soon as it is worn. Do-it-yourself enthusiasts will be

BELOW: *A ginger cat makes use of a rough bark scratching post to stretch its limbs and sharpen its claws simultaneously.*

CAT TOYS

For rolling and chasing: ping-pong balls, plastic lemons, wine corks, pine cones, catnip scented 'mice' from pet shops, pens and pencils to be batted onto hard flooring.

For jumping and pouncing: aluminium foil ball or feather on a string dangled in the air, dressing-gown cord or cotton reel on string pulled slowly along floor.

For ambush: strong paper bags, cardboard boxes, old blanket scrunched up in a heap.

RIGHT: *Cats soon learn to use a cat flap with great confidence and no doubt enjoy the independence that it brings.*

able to construct a post, though you must be careful to fix it to a stable base so that it will not wobble or fall over when the cat gets to work.

CAT-FLAPS

Feelings for and against cat-flaps run high amongst owners. *For* is the convenience of not having to open the door every 10 minutes and the pleasure it gives the cat when it can come and go as it pleases. *Against* is the likelihood that the cat will bring in its prey (dead or alive), the certainty of muddy pawmarks on your floors and the possibility that other cats will make use of the flap and arrive unannounced. There is also the problem that, much of the time, you will not know whether your cat is out or in.

The most useful type of cat-flap has a clear plastic door, so that the cat can see where it is going and what awaits on the other side, has a magnetic strip along the sides to keep out draughts and an either-way locking device. The lock means that you can fasten the door shut at night, allow the cat to come in but not go out, and vice versa. Check that the flap is easy to push and will not snap back too hard and trap a paw - a side opening may be more suitable - and that it opens quickly to give the cat a speedy escape route from a trespassing dog. If there are other cats in the neighbourhood, you might prefer the type of flap activated by a magnetic collar so that it will only open for your own cat.

The flap should be fitted near enough to the base of the door for the cat to step through rather than jump. If this means that it is within an arm's reach of the doorlock, fit a higher lock. Many a spur-of-the-moment burglar has been tempted by a cat-flap and a lock within reach seals the crime.

When training the cat to use its new exit, start near the cat's mealtime, propping the flap open but make sure that it is secure: if it bangs down on the cat's head on the first foray, the cat may avoid it forever more. Probably the smell of the outdoors will be enough but if it simply sits and looks at the opening, go outside and tempt it through with a tidbit. Then close the flap and shortly afterwards put the cat's meal within sight inside and tap the bowl to attract its attention. Some cats are very suspicious of the flap and refuse to attempt to push it. In this case you may have to prop open the flap for a time each day until the cat is going to and fro happily and enjoying its new freedom. Then hold the flap halfway open so that it can put its head through. When it is halfway through, let the door fall gently, so that the cat gets used to the feel of the flap resting on its back and the noise it makes when it falls back. You should be able to open the flap a little less each time until the cat realizes that it is safe to push through on its own.

COLLARS

Like cat-flaps, collars are regarded as a necessity by some owners, while others are set against them. A collar with an identity tag bearing your phone number will mean that your cat can be returned home if it roams too far and that you can be notified immediately if it is injured in an accident. However, there is always the danger that the collar will get caught on a branch or fence and the cat will be unable to get free. For this reason the collar should always have an elastic strip, to enable the cat to wriggle out but even with this safeguard, many a cat has hanged itself on its collar. You can minimize the risk by cutting part-way through the elastic so that it will break at any sharp tug,

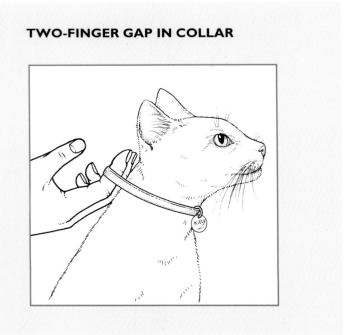

TWO-FINGER GAP IN COLLAR

and be prepared to replace the collar often! When fitting the collar, you should be able to insert one finger between the collar and the cat's neck. If there is room for two fingers, the collar is too loose.

Some breeds take well to walking on a leash and will walk daintily down the street with you like a small dog. This particularly applies to Siamese, Burmese, Russian Blue and Foreigns, but it is surprisingly easy to train any cat to accept a leash - providing you are willing to go where the cat goes. This can be extremely useful for owners who want to allow their cats to prowl round the garden but are worried about them roaming further. An occasional cat will accept a collar and leash but most will react with panic to a tug on the neck, so a harness is much more suitable. Use the type that buckles round the neck and chest rather than the elasticated type that is easier to slip on but far from secure: if an uncooperative cat chooses to back away from you, a slight tug on the leash will bring the elasticated harness straight over the cat's head.

Begin by leaving the harness near the cat's bed for a couple of days so that the cat can inspect it and it will bear a reassuring smell. Then put it on for the first time during a play session, leave it on for a few minutes while you do your best to distract the cat with a game, then remove it. The cat may do everything possible to get free of the harness in the meantime, but when you repeat the process the next day, it will probably react far more calmly. Once the cat is used to the harness, attach a light leather or cord leash and let it trail around on the floor at first. The cat will soon be using the leash for chasing and pouncing games, but don't let it out of your sight, as the leash may catch on something and undo all your good work. Next, hold the leash loosely and sit down a short way from your cat. Put its favourite food treat in front of you then give a gentle tug on the leash, just enough for the cat to notice, but *don't* haul it towards you. With a bit of luck the cat will advance towards the food.

Try a few walks around the house before you go out of doors. Always act quietly and gently and remember that you will never persuade a cat to go anywhere against its will.

ABOVE: *An outdoor run gives the best of both worlds: the security of indoors and the air, light, smells and excitement of the garden.*

INDOOR AND OUTDOOR CATS

Many owners feel that roaming freely is so much part of the cat's nature that it is cruel to keep them indoors. However, more and more people, recognizing that indoor cats have a longer life expectancy, are opting for keeping their cat confined. A cat used to outdoor freedom would certainly feel deprived if it suddenly found that it could only view the world through a window, but cats that spend their whole lives indoors seem to accept their lot quite happily and would be terrified if they suddenly found themselves outside. Outdoor cats can enjoy the pleasures of hunting but they are also exposed to the dangers of traffic, aggressive dogs and fighting cats, as well as being far more likely to pick up diseases. If you have a small town garden, in an area where it would be dangerous for the cat to roam further, don't simply rely on 'keeping an eye' on your cat when it is outside. It only takes a couple of seconds for the cat to take fright at a noise and be over the wall and away and there is nothing you can do about it.

Indoor cats obviously have fewer opportunities for amusing themselves than their outdoor cousins, so they need companionship. It is not fair to leave a cat shut indoors all day, every day, if the whole family is out at work. Even when human company is usually available, it is kinder to keep two cats. They

OPPOSITE: *Most cats take to being walked in a harness relatively well provided it is introduced in a sensitive way.*

OPPOSITE: *Outdoor cats can enjoy the pleasures of tree climbing and hunting but are also exposed to the dangers of neighbouring cats, aggressive dogs and infectious diseases.*

RIGHT: *Indoor cats often start nibbling the houseplants for amusement so make sure that the ones you have are harmless to animals.*

will get extra exercise from chasing one another and at meal-times the competitive spirit will stimulate their appetites. Play sessions are especially important for keeping indoor cats in good condition. Ask your veterinarian about mineral supplements: some cats living indoors become deficient in vitamin D which is obtained from direct sunlight; sun coming through glass does not have the same effect.

You can give your cat the best of both worlds by fixing up an outside run, which you can buy in a self-assembly kit in a wide range of sizes. Unless the cat has free access to and from the run through a cat-flap, you should provide water and a litter tray and there should always be a shady section for the cat to hide if it is feeling the heat. Alternatively, you might consider surrounding your garden with a high mesh fence with a top that slopes inwards at a 45° angle, which prevents your cat climbing out. It is a safe solution although rarely pleasing to gardeners.

CATS AND PLANTS

Many plants, both outdoor and indoor, contain chemicals that are poisonous to cats. Plenty of cats seem to know instinctively that they must steer clear of potentially harmful plants and co-exist quite happily with them throughout their lives. However, if your cat is a chronic nibbler, champing indiscriminately at

POTENTIALLY HARMFUL PLANTS:

IN THE GARDEN: autumn crocus, azalea, bird of paradise, bleeding heart, broom, burning bush, buttercup, cherry laurel, Christmas rose, cornflower, crocus, daffodil, foxglove, holly, horse chestnut, hyacinth, iris, ivy, laburnum, laurel, lily of the valley, lupin, mistletoe, peach, rhododendron, wisteria, yew.

IN THE HOUSE: azalea, cyclamen, dieffenbachia, hyacinth, philodendron, poinsettia.

CATNIP

Catnip (*Nepeta cataria*) is a herb that gives cats a 'high'. Just a pinch of the dried variety obtainable from pet shops - sprinkled on their bedding, has them sniffing, rubbing their face against it and rolling about in ecstasy. The reason is a chemical contained in catnip that works on the cat's nervous system; it is harmless and non-additive and gives your pet 15 minutes of pure bliss. Commercially produced cat toys are impregnated with catnip, but the effect soon wears off. If you keep dried catnip in an airtight jar and seal the toy inside overnight, then bring it out as a special treat; your cat will be overjoyed.

everything in sight, then it is only sensible to remove the poisonous varieties from the garden. Indoor cats often turn to houseplants in moments of boredom, so if you must keep the suspect varieties, put them well out of the cat's reach or keep the cat out of rooms where they are growing.

If your cat is permanently indoors and shows an interest in browsing on every available plant, you might consider growing a special window box with safe and delectable plants like parsley, sage, wheat or oats as well as grass (see Chapter 3).

CHILDREN AND CATS

Cats and children can get along very well together, providing the children are taught a few simple rules and never allowed to think of the cat as a cuddly toy to be squeezed and hauled about

BABY SENSE

- ❧ Never leave the baby and cat alone together: make sure that they are supervised at all times.

- ❧ Always keep a net over the baby's pram or crib in case the cat decides to share it.

- ❧ Never let a baby (or any child) near the litter tray. Perhaps you can find a place on a cupboard, out of the baby's reach.

- ❧ Always keep the cat well away from the baby's food, both at preparation and feeding times.

BELOW: *When shown how to handle cats properly, children can learn to look after their pets very satisfactorily.*

as the whim takes them. Even babies can be guided to stroke a cat with the flat of the palm, to gurgles of delight on one side and happy purring on the other. Toddlers can be shown how to make friends with a cat, holding out a hand for the introductory sniff, then waiting for the cat to make friendly overtures before beginning to stroke and rub round its ears, along its back and at the base of the tail, leaving the tummy and back legs alone. They should understand that the cat must not be disturbed when it is eating, sleeping or using the litter tray and it is probably best to teach young children not to pick up the cat at all. They usually hold them too tightly, hang onto them when they struggle and try to carry them round like babies, with their tummies uppermost and their paws in the air. Some cats will put up with this kind of treatment but most will protest vigorously and your child may end up scratched or bitten.

RE-TRAINING A CAT

When an adult cat arrives in your household, you will want to train it to your ways, as far as possible. It is much safer to keep your cat indoors at night but if at its previous home it was accustomed to roaming free after dark, it will probably object strenuously at first. The golden rule is: don't weaken. Give the cat plenty of fuss and feed it a special treat last thing, then shut it in the kitchen (or whatever room you choose) with a litter tray and its favourite toys. Put in your earplugs and resolutely ignore all miaowing and scratching until morning. So long as you stick to your plan without weakening, re-training will be much quicker than you imagine.

If your cat has always used a litter tray in the past but you would prefer it to 'go' outside, begin by putting the litter tray near the door, then (on fine days) put it just outside, either leaving the door open or opening it at the appropriate times. Once the cat is used to the new arrangement, move the tray to a nearby patch of earth in a quiet place, then, a couple of days later, remove the tray altogether but leave a scattering of used litter on the earth.

GROOMING

Cats are naturally clean animals and spend a good part of the day grooming themselves, their rough tongues acting as brush and comb to clean the coat and remove dead hair. Self-grooming also removes 'foreign' smells from the coat - a cat will usually have a good wash after being handled by a stranger - and helps to cool them in hot weather.

ABOVE: *In the same way that cats which are used to running free outdoors can be taught to stay indoors for certain periods, so too can 'indoor' cats gradually be trained to enjoy excursions outside.*

Long-haired cats need daily help in grooming, otherwise they will ingest too much hair, their fur will become tangled and, in the last resort, matted lumps will have to be shaved off by the veterinarian under anaesthetic. Short-haired cats can get along with very little extra grooming but a weekly session will keep them looking good and mean less discarded hair on your furniture. Even shorthairs, kept in centrally-heated homes, lose an amazing amount of hair. Some cats enjoy grooming so much that they come scampering at the tap of a comb while others fight all the way *(see pages 62-63).*

GROOMING ROUTINE FOR LONGHAIRS

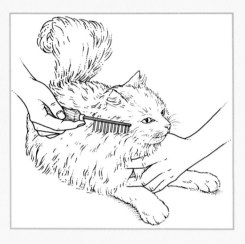

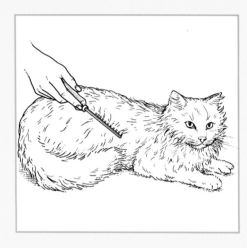

STEP 1 Start combing with a wide-toothed comb around the head and neck, where the cat enjoys it most.

STEP 2 Move to the legs, then raise the cat on its hind legs to comb the abdomen and the underparts of the 'trousers'. If you find tangles, sprinkle with a little non-scented talcum powder and tease them out with your fingers. Once the wide-toothed comb goes through easily, change to a fine-toothed comb.

STEP 3 Work along the back and sides, combing in an upwards direction to fluff out the hairs. Start at the hind end and work towards the head.

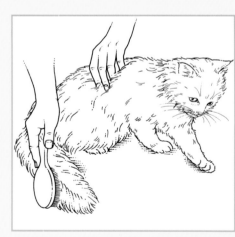

STEP 4 Using a wire brush, brush the fur vigorously the 'wrong' way, working from head to tail, then brush with the lie of the hair.

STEP 6 Brush out the hair around the neck into a ruff, so that you have started and finished the brush-comb routine in the cat's favourite spot.

STEP 7 Use a damp pad of cotton wool to wipe round each eye. Sometimes blocked tear ducts cause discoloration round the eyes of long-haired cats and this can be removed with a mild salt solution.

STEP 5 Make a parting down the tail and brush out the hair on one side, then the other.

STEP 8 Moisten a pad of cotton wool with baby oil or olive oil to remove dirt from the outer cup of the ear but never poke anything into the ear itself.

GROOMING ROUTINE FOR SHORTHAIRS

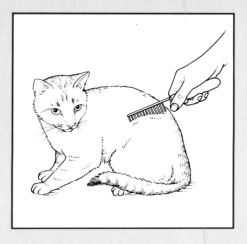

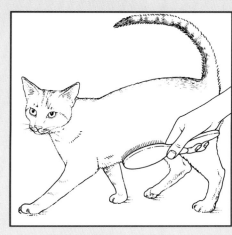

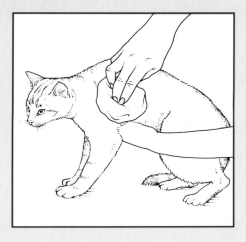

STEP 1 Comb with a fine-toothed comb, starting round the head and under the chin, then working along from head to tail.

STEP 2 Use a bristle brush to remove the dead hair and stand the cat on its hindlegs to brush the chest and tummy. A rubber brush is more suitable for Rex cats as it is less likely to scratch.

STEP 3 Rub with a chamois leather to bring out the shine of the coat.

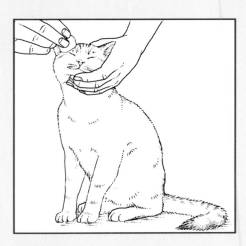

STEP 4 Wipe around each eye with a damp pad of cotton wool.

In between grooming sessions, stroking is an excellent method of removing dead hair.

STEP 5 If necessary, use a cotton wool pad moistened with baby oil or olive oil to remove dirt from the outer cup of the ear but do not poke inside the ear itself.

BATHING A CAT

Unless you are showing a cat, bathing should be considered only as a last resort in an emergency, for example if your cat has managed to roll in a patch of oil or grease. Most cats hate to get their fur wet and get into quite a panic the moment washing begins *(see page 65)*.

RIGHT: *These healthy kittens are probably the best of friends, but when food is around animals often become quite boisterous.*

TRIMMING THE CLAWS

 Use sharp clippers specially designed for the job and available from pet shops. Don't use ordinary scissors, which may splinter the claw.

 Press the pads of the paw gently, so that the claws are exposed.

 Cut only the white tips, which are dead tissue. The cat may not enjoy the procedure but it will not be hurt. Never touch the pink quick within the claw as this will result in pain and bleeding.

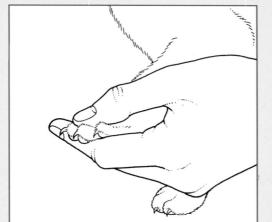

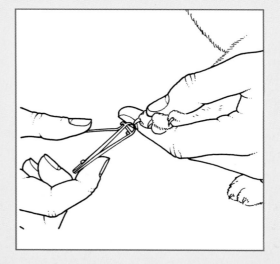

BATHING A CAT

STEP 1 Make certain that you have everything you need within arm's reach: special cat shampoo (don't use shampoo meant for humans), jug for rinsing, several towels, comb.

STEP 2 Fill the sink or a large bowl with warm water to a depth of about 10cm (4in). The sink may be more convenient as it is at waist height but you might find a rubber mat useful to stop the cat skidding about. If you put a bowl on a table, then a mat beneath it may prevent the whole thing from ending up on the floor.

STEP 3 Test the temperature of the water: it should be about blood heat, no hotter.

STEP 4 Lift in the cat and use the jug to wet its fur, starting from the back and ending at the neck.

STEP 5 Once the fur is wet, gently massage in the shampoo, taking care not to let it near the ears or eyes.

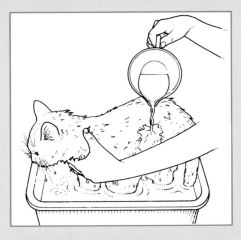

STEP 6 Keep rinsing with warm water until all traces of shampoo are gone.

STEP 10 When the fur is completely dry, comb it through.

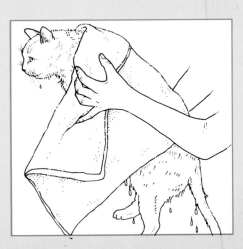

STEP 7 Lift out the cat and wrap it in a warm, dry towel.

STEP 8 Gently clean round the face with a soft, damp cloth.

STEP 9 If the cat will allow it, dry the fur with a hair drier on a low setting, brushing the hair gently at the same time. If your cat is scared of the hair drier, rub it as dry as you can, then wrap it in another warm, dry towel. Keep it in a warm room for the rest of the day and overnight.

If your cat looks a little grubby from time to time, especially if it is getting old and does not have the energy to wash properly, you might try a dry shampooing technique. For a pale coloured cat use a plain, unscented talcum powder. Rub it into the coat, then comb and brush thoroughly until all traces are removed. For a darker coloured cat use bran (the type you sprinkle on your cereal for extra fibre). Heat it in the oven until it is warm - *not hot* - then proceed as with talcum powder.

Chapter 6
SOLVING BEHAVIOUR PROBLEMS

Cats are much more trainable than many owners realize and if behaviour problems

do arise, they can often be dealt with quite simply, so long as you take the time

to see the world from your cat's point of view.

SPRAYING

Cats can often be seen backing up to a bush in the garden and, from a standing position, spraying a small jet of urine backwards. Both sexes spray and neutered males are just as likely to spray as unneutered toms, though a tom's urine will be more smelly. Normally, cats do not feel the need to spray indoors as they are secure and there is no need to protect the territory against invaders, though when several cats share a house, each may mark out its own patch. If your cat suddenly starts spraying your curtains and chair legs, look for some change in the household that has put it under stress (see below). A common cause is the installation of a cat-flap. For some cats this blurs the distinction between indoors and outdoors and they need to boost their confidence by increasing the intensity of their own smell.

Some owners scatter pepper or chilli or wipe the sprayed areas with vinegar as deterrents, but this seldom works. You might try placing a tray of marbles below the favourite spraying places but a determined sprayer may simply stand further away. A sheet of household foil wrapped round chosen spot may do the trick, as cats dislike the sound of urine spraying onto foil.

The psychological approach may be more successful. If you have more than two cats, try giving each one a separate room – or at best a completely separate place – to sleep in. If your neighbour's cat is always prowling round outside and trying to slip in through the kitchen door, chase it away. If you have installed a cat-flap recently, try boarding it up and see if the behaviour stops. In difficult cases, confine the cat to one room when unsupervised and make sure it has a cosy bed in a warm spot, perhaps under a radiator, and its favourite toys. So long as you don't leave it alone long enough to feel neglected, its sense of security should increase; when it no longer feels the need to spray in the one room, let it use more of the house, but keep an eye on it for the time being. If none of these strategies work, your veterinarian may advise hormone treatment.

OPPOSITE: *Cats of both sexes sometimes start spraying when they feel unsure of themselves for some reason. By establishing a sense of their own smell, their confidence is boosted.*

ABOVE: *Lovers of routine, cats often react to changes in their surroundings by spraying.*

CATS UNDER STRESS

Cats love the safety of routine and any change in their familiar surroundings or the behaviour of their owners can cause stress which shows itself in various ways: it may avoid petting, eat poorly or begin spraying or soiling.

Among the stress-bringing changes are:

Guests in the house
Death in the family
Redecoration or new furniture
A new baby
The arrival of a new pet
Marriage breakup

SOILING

Soiling may be caused by the same upsets as spraying but it can also be the first sign of illness, so a veterinary checkup is advisable. It may be that the cat has a bladder problem or is suffering from constipation, so that it has begun to associate the litter tray with pain and discomfort. Some cats do begin to soil because they are allergic to something in their food or to some chemical used in the home, so if you have changed the cat's diet, used carpet shampoo or even repainted the kitchen, the explanation may be simple.

In some cases the cat may be asking, in the only way it can, for the litter tray to be changed more often, or it may be unhappy with the type of litter used. Try a finer-grained litter, or stop using those with a deodorant added. Other possibilities are that the tray is placed too near to the cat's food or in a high-traffic area where feet constantly tramp past. If lack of peace and privacy could be the problem, a hooded litter tray may be the solution.

Never smack or scold a cat for soiling, even if you catch it in the act; this will increase any feelings of insecurity and make the behaviour worse. The old idea of rubbing the cat's nose in the mess is even more counter-productive; probably the cat will enjoy the smell and want more of it. Instead, begin by cleaning the area thoroughly with a warm solution of biological detergent, followed by surgical spirit, or with a weak solution of household bleach, and a scattering of baking soda. In both cases, check your fabrics for colour fastness first. Don't use any disinfectant containing chlorine or ammonia; it may smell clean and fresh to you but to a cat it smells as though another cat has been in the house and draws it back to the place. Some disinfectants can also be absorbed through the paws.

Discourage the cat from revisiting the soiled area by laying a sheet of slightly crinkled aluminium foil over it or try feeding the cat in that place, once it is completely clean. No cat will soil its feeding place. If the cat tends to leave a deposit in the middle of your bed - this seems to be a favourite location if the cat is upset at being left alone too long or left behind while the family go on holiday - fix a sheet of plastic over the bed.

BELOW: *Once security is re-established, behavioural problems will usually disappear.*

SCRATCHING FURNITURE

Scratching is natural behaviour for the cat but will be unaccept-able if it ruins your expensive furniture. The first essential is to give the cat a good scratching post (see Chapter 5) of its own. To begin with, position the post in front of the favourite area for scratching and rub some dried catnip into it as an extra incentive. As the cat gets used to using the post, gradually move it towards its permanent position. If the cat then uses the post *and* your best armchair, you will have to employ deterrent methods. The simplest is to wrap a piece of plastic round the scratched corner, as cats dislike the feel of plastic under their paws. If your fabric will take it, an alternative is a couple of strips of double-sided sticky tape, which are guaranteed to dis-courage the cat.

A more elaborate deterrent is the balloon method. Buy a packet of balloons and sit on the floor blowing them up. The cat will soon come over to see what you are doing. Once it begins to sniff at the balloon, burst one in front of it. Repeat this a couple of times until the cat realizes that balloons are bad news, then attach a couple to the scratched area of furniture. The cat will walk round them warily and you can remove them after a week or two, when the habit has been broken. Any of the deterrent methods may have to be reinforced from time to time, if the cat goes back to its old ways.

Fabric eating

Many young cats, particularly Siamese and Burmese, suck or chew wool, probably as an extension of their infant suckling activities and they may go on to eat all sorts of fabrics, ruining any jumpers, towels, sheets and cushion covers they can get between their teeth. This is more common among indoor cats and can sometimes be a sign of boredom. You may be able to cut down on the chewing by spending more time playing with your cat or taking it out in the harness and leash. Even better, erect an outside run which could give it access to grass and herbs.

ABOVE RIGHT: *Kittens will be distracted from gnawing your flower supports if you provide them with their own scratching post.*

OPPOSITE: *Fabric chewing is often associated with boredom, so one solution is to provide distractions in the form of homemade cloth toys, for example.*

DECLAWING

Declawing is a surgical procedure which removes the cat's claws, along with part of the base of the toes. It is accepted in the U.S. as a method of protecting the owner's furniture but in the U.K. veterinarians will perform the operation only in cases of injury or disease. The U.K. view is that such a painful mutilation, simply for the owner's convenience, is unthinkable. It leaves a cat unable to climb or protect itself and can be so traumatic that a cat's personality is permanently affected.

Try increasing the fibre content of the cat's diet, adding a little bran to each meal and also sharing a little of your cooked vegetables - potatoes, carrots, cauliflower or mushrooms. Many cats will enjoy a spoonful of high-fibre breakfast cereal with their canned food.

BITING AND SCRATCHING

It is unusual for cats to be aggressive towards people unless they are unwisely handled, but if they have not had enough human contact and petting as kittens they may develop what is known as the 'petting and biting syndrome'. One minute your cat is sitting quietly on your lap, purring and giving every appearance of enjoying your stroking hand, then the next minute it fastens its front claws into your hand and sinks its teeth into your flesh, while its back claws beat painfully at your arm. It seems that at first your cat is revelling in kitten behaviour, being cuddled and mothered, then suddenly it reverts to adulthood and feels trapped and panicky, so it needs to strike out in self-defence. If this happens, limit yourself to short sessions of petting your cat for the time being. When it sits on your lap don't cradle it with your arms, but leave it free to get down as soon as it wants. Don't try to rub its tummy or touch its back legs and after a few minutes, put it down. Probably your cat will want to initiate more contact and its moments of feeling under threat will become less frequent.

PETTING AND BITING SYNDROME

One minute your cat seems to be enjoying your caresses and the next minute it has your fingers in a vice-like grip.

If your normally docile pet has suddenly turned aggressive, it could be an allergic reaction. If you are using any new household cleansers, stop using them for a week and see if your cat calms down. If you have had your chairs, carpet or curtains cleaned, try excluding the cat from that room for a time. You might also try a gradual change of diet, perhaps feeding fresh fish or chicken instead of canned food, at least until you see whether this makes a difference. Even if a cat has been fed on a particular brand of canned food for years, the recipe may have changed slightly to include an additive which causes an allergic reaction in your particular cat.

A cat that fastens its claws into your ankles every time you pass, pounces on your moving hand with claws outstretched (cats normally sheath their claws for a friendly pounce) or becomes overexcited in play and inflicts minor wounds, may not have enough action and stimulation in its life. If possible, give it more opportunity to go outside, even if you have to take it on a harness. Half an hour a day of chase and pounce games, using a cotton-reel or 'mouse' on a string may well do wonders.

OVER-GROOMING

Apart from self-grooming to clean and condition itself, you will probably see your cat grooming itself if it has been startled or threatened in some way; the action is obviously soothing and relaxing. In very highly-strung cats, or those under great stress, this can turn into self-mutilation, where the cat actually pulls out lumps of hair, or licks so long and hard that bald patches appear on its legs, tummy, flanks or the base of the tail.

In some cases the answer may be more human companionship, more play or a new feline playmate. In the early stages, try to distract the cat by banging something on the table or using a jet of plain water from a water pistol, but if none of this works your veterinarian might prescribe sedatives or suggest the use of an Elizabethan collar for a while.

AVERSION TO VISITORS

Some nervous cats regard any visitor to the home as an unwelcome intruder. They either disappear and go into hiding until the strangers have left or slink around behind the furniture glowering suspiciously at everyone. The simplest way to tackle this behaviour is to ignore it. Tell your visitors that it's nothing personal, this is a one-person cat and they should pay no attention to its unfriendly glare. The cat may lose its dislike of visi-

ABOVE: *An Elizabethan collar prevents the cat from licking its wound. The device is also sometimes used on cats which over-groom.*

tors with time, but you should on no account pull it out of its hiding place and hold it up for introductions. This will confirm all its worst fears and ensure that it will bolt in future, so that this distressing experience cannot be repeated.

If you long for a more sociable cat and are determined to do something about it, you must be prepared to take time and trouble. When visitors arrive, put the cat in its carrier in a quiet corner. Look after your visitor and ignore the cat completely for 15 minutes or so, then remove the cat, still in its carrier, and put it in another room. Only release it half an hour later, when you give it a tidbit and a lot of fuss. Each time visitors come, increase the time the cat spends with you, in its carrier. It will gradually come to realize that visitors mean it no harm and its

73

ABOVE: *Over-dependence, although rewarding in some ways, can become overbearing. Sensitive training will cure your cat of following you like a shadow.*

OPPOSITE: *Cats which are not handled frequently and those which have been roughly treated can grow up wary of humans.*

fears are groundless. Once it stops looking wild and terrified you can open the carrier door after the first few minutes. Let the cat takes its time to choose when to come out and school your visitors to look the other way unless and until the cat makes friendly overtures in their direction.

OVER-ATTACHMENT

Of course you like your cat to show affection, but it can be both irritating and worrying when it follows you everywhere, tripping you up, jumping on your lap the moment you sit down and working itself into a nervous state every time you go shopping. Cats sometimes become too attached to their owners if they are kept indoors and are dependent on them for interest and company. The eventual answer may be a feline companion but if you introduce a second pet before you have weaned your cat from its over-dependence, it will probably feel jealous and resentful and you will be no further on.

You must school your cat to do without you, so don't let it follow you from room to room. Shut it out of the kitchen when you are preparing meals or out of the study when you are working. It will probably stand outside the door mewing piteously, but you will have to steel yourself. Don't let it settle on your lap for the whole evening, so that you are pinned down in one place. After a few minutes, put it on the floor, give it a quick stroke, then go and do something else. The cat should not be made to feel that it is being punished – only that it has to get used to periods of separation. Set aside times when you give the cat a short, intense session of cuddling and petting, so that these replace the clinging over-dependence.

UNDER-DEPENDENCE

Some cats seem to be born with a great need for contact with humans, while others are independent and require far less petting. But, given this basic difference in temperament, what happens to the kitten in the first few weeks of life is vital for the cat's later development. If it is not handled frequently by humans, or if it is roughly treated, it may grow up wary and anti-social, avoiding a stroking hand or stiffening up when held. You will need to be patient in building up the relationship and let the cat come to you in its own good time.

Feed the cat little and often, holding out the dish and encouraging it to follow you. Either squat down beside the cat while it eats, stroking it occasionally and talking to it gently, or put the

ABOVE: *Resentment at the introduction of a young newcomer is understand-able and needs delicate handling by the owner to prevent it escalating.*

food bowl on a table and sit alongside. Don't put the cat on your lap but put the catnip mouse there so that the cat has to climb over you to seize it. If the cat has a favourite chair, make a habit of sitting in it, then when the cat decides to join you, let it settle with no fuss beyond a quiet word and a gentle stroke. If your cat usually spreads itself out in front of the fire or next to the radiator, try lying down there yourself. Once you are right down to their level, most cats overcome their timidity and begin to give an interested sniff, which invites a friendly over-ture. Slowly attachment will grow.

RESENTMENT OF NEWCOMER

Most cats will adapt to a newcomer, once they understand that their position in the household is unaffected, and indeed a com-panion may solve many problems, as explained above. However, in some cases the hostility persists and becomes a problem. It may show itself in growling and hissing, stand-offs

and scuffling every time the cats meet. The dominant cat may indulge in mounting and napebiting or the long-time resident may undergo a character change, no longer greeting the owner and showing affection, but taking off by itself for long periods.

Try letting the new cat out in the mornings and keeping the established car indoors with you, talking to it, fussing it and let-ting it feel special. In the afternoon, let that cat out and keep the other one in, giving it plenty of fuss. If you are out all day, or the cats live indoors, work out some way of giving each cat its own time with you. Reunite the cats at mealtimes, feeding them side by side, as this is often the first step towards a friendly relationship.

If the newcomer is a kitten, an adult cat probably finds its energy and playfulness a nuisance and it may be a relief when the kitten grows up and becomes a little more staid. With two adult cats, the process of adjustment may take a long time and some cats, like some humans, will never become friends, though they should learn to rub along together.

OPPOSITE: *The process of adjustment may take some time but, more often than not, two cats in the same household soon become firm friends.*

Chapter 7
YOUR CAT ON THE MOVE

Cats prefer familiar routine on their own territory. If they become convinced that every trip in the carrier or car

ends in a strange-smelling room where a man in a white coat sticks needles into them, it's not surprising

that they try to fight off any attempt at removal.

However, if they get used to excursions and learn that there are normally no nasty surprises at the end of them and sometimes even nice ones, you should have no trouble beyond the occasional complaint about confinement.

CHOOSING AND USING CARRIERS

The first requirement for any journey is a secure carrier. They come in all shapes and sizes and some cats feel safer in the closed-in type while others like to see everything that is happening around them. It makes sense to buy a good quality carrier which will give you many years of service. Even if you do not plan to take your cats on holiday, you will need it more often than you think. Though you can buy a cheap cardboard version which can be useful for an emergency, for example if you have to collect an unexpected feline visitor at short notice, a determined cat will claw its way out and the cardboard will begin to disintegrate if it vomits or urinates. Also, most cats find being enclosed in the dark very frightening.

Plastic-coated wire carriers are very durable, easy to clean and disinfect and have the advantage of allowing the cat to see out in all directions. The extra ventilation is useful in summer but in winter you may need to cover the top with a blanket. A nervous cat may prefer the somewhat less robust fibre-glass alternative with a plastic-coated wire door so that it will feel well-protected while still being able to peer out at the world. Wicker carriers are available and cats enjoy chewing them but they have the same disadvantages as wicker beds and the door is fastened with straps, which can become worn and present a security hazard if the door is attacked by a large and angry cat. Closed-in carriers can become very hot if you are travelling in midsummer and on sunny days you may need to lay a damp cloth over the top.

Don't make the mistake of buying a kitten-sized carrier, only to find that your cat outgrows it. If you have no idea how large your cat will grow, buy a carrier that would accommodate

OPPOSITE: *A wicker basket with a plastic-coated wire door provides a very acceptable travelling device for a young ginger cat.*

ABOVE: *Allow your kittens time to get used to the basket and to explore it inside and out before confining them in it.*

jumbo-size if necessary. It is easier to lift a reluctant cat in and out of a top-opening rather than front-opening carrier, but check that the lid is firmly anchored to the frame on one side, and has a foolproof fastening on the other side. If not, then a moment's carelessness can result in a terrified cat escaping and streaking off down a busy street.

Well before a journey, leave the carrier out, its door open and a toy inside, so that the cat can explore it. If you leave some bedding inside at night, it might enjoy trying out a new sleeping place and by the time you are ready to travel, the carrier should hold no fears.

CAR TRAVEL

Always keep your cat in its carrier on car journeys. Leaving a cat free within the car is very dangerous, even if it is docile enough to drape itself over the back shelf in the sunshine. All sorts of sudden noises, or an emergency stop, may startle the cat and cause it to land, claws outstretched, on the driver's neck. Cats have been known to wiggle through an impossible-looking gap in a window while the driver asks for directions. Holding a cat, however well-trained, on harness and leash during the journey is risky; if there was an accident the cat might well flee in terror, leash and all.

If your cat is prone to car sickness, then it should have no food for three or four hours before the journey but other cats may settle better if their mealtime routine is not disrupted. Sprinkle a little catnip in the carrier, give it a favourite toy to cuddle and,

CAT MINDERS

In most areas there are professional 'minders' who will come to your home each day and feed your cat while you are on holiday. If you are thinking of employing a minder, be sure to take precautions.

* Ask for and follow up at least two references. The minder must be experienced with cats, thoroughly reliable and honest.

* Check how often the minder will visit and how much time he/she will spend with the cat.

* Ask what arrangements will be made if the minder falls ill.

* Give the minder a full list of the cat's feeding and other requirements.

* Leave your veterinarian's number and an emergency contact number.

* If possible arrange for a neighbour to look in every couple of days to check that all is well. Leave an emergency contact number with the neighbour too.

* Remove your valuables from the house to avoid possible temptation.

with luck, the gentle motion of the car will soon make it drowsy. On a very long journey, take along a litter tray, water and a bowl and every three hours or so, pull into a quiet spot, make certain doors and windows are firmly shut and let the cat out to have a drink, use the tray and stretch its legs. Then put it back in the carrier before you clear up and continue your journey.

If every journey sends your cat into a frenzy, you may be able to obtain a sedative from your veterinarian, but most are reluctant to prescribe them, as they can make some cats even more excitable, instead of having the expected calming effect. If you are using them for the first time, try them out before the journey to test the effect on your cat. But in any case, don't judge by the first journey. A cat may howl and hurl itself against the sides of the carrier, with every sign of great distress, on the first or even the second journey, then next time settle down peacefully, without a sign of anxiety.

Never leave your cat in a parked car on a hot day, whether or not the windows are open for ventilation. It may be very ill by

RIGHT: *If you are leaving the cat at home in the care of a neighbour or minder, ensure that the cat's welfare is foremost in the carer's mind and avoid a situation in which the cat remains alone for long periods.*

the time you get back. For safety's sake, it is better not to leave cats unattended in the car at any time. If your car is stolen, the thief is unlikely to give a good home to your cat and it may be dumped on the roadside.

BOARDING YOUR CAT

If you have no willing neighbour or family to give your cat proper care while you are on holiday, a boarding cattery may be the only practical answer. Personal recommendations are best, so ask around among cat-owners and the local veterinarians, but don't rely on that for making your choice. Always inspect a cattery yourself and ask plenty of questions. If you are not welcome to inspect the entire premises (and preferably twice, at different times of day) and if your questions are not fully and satisfactorily answered, take your business elsewhere. Any good cattery will insist that all guests have up to date inoculations and you should not consider leaving your cat with any boarding establishment that does not follow this rule. The points you will want to check fall into four main categories.

Safety

* The accommodation must have a double door system, so that if a cat escapes from one section, it cannot get out of the unit.
* Built-in heating should be used, with no free-standing units.
* Multiple accommodation should have more than one exit, in case of fire.
* Fire extinguishers and sand buckets should be provided.
* There should be a strict 'no smoking' rule for staff and visitors as much of the cat's furniture - baskets, boxes, bedding - is highly inflammable.

Comfort

* Whatever the design of the cattery, the cat must have a snug and peaceful place to sleep.
* Most cats will need an outside run, unless they are used to a permanent indoor life. If it is roofed, the cat will be able to use it rain or shine.
* A shelf to sit on and watch the world go by will keep the cat from becoming bored.
* A scratching post will contribute to the cat's feeling of wellbeing.
* The accommodation should be airy and well-ventilated and not sited in a damp or shady area.
* If dogs are also boarded, they should be well away from the cats so that cats are not upset by constant barking.

Hygiene

* Beds should be disposable or easily disinfected.
* Food should not be left down long after mealtimes.
* There should be clean water in each pen at all times.

BELOW: *After moving to a new home, cats tend to be timid in the first few days and rarely venture far from the house.*

★ Runs should be concrete, not grass.

★ Pens should never be sited on top of one another.

★ Ideally, runs should be separated by as much as a metre (yard) but, failing that, sneeze barriers should be in place to prevent cats meeting face to face.

★ All surfaces must be easily cleanable with no dirt-trapping corners.

★ Only cats from the same family should share runs.

Care

★ Good cattery proprietors should love cats and demonstrate a real interest in their boarders as they show you round.

★ They should want to know about your cat's likes and dislikes and be willing to feed a special diet if necessary.

★ They should be willing to let you take along your cat's bedding and toys so that it will feel at home.

★ When you leave your cat, you will normally be asked to sign a form authorizing any necessary treatment and to leave your veterinarian's number and an emergency number where you, or someone who could act on your behalf, can be contacted.

On first arrival, your cat may be very upset and nervous but on your return you will (if you have chosen your cattery carefully) be surprised at how well it has settled in. Subsequent visits will be much less traumatic: the cat will remember both the place and the people.

MOVING HOUSE

A house full of strange men humping furniture is a bad scene for a cat and the best idea is to confine it in the bathroom, where it can be left undisturbed with its bed, food, water and litter tray. Once the house is quiet, put the cat in its carrier and give it a treat. Along with your cat's furniture, take a little used litter as it will provide a reassuring smell. At the new house, give the cat a treat as it leaves the carrier and confine it again, until all bewildering activity has stopped. The bathroom is a good choice because it will be reasonably peaceful and have few escape routes. Frightened cats have been known to try to scramble up chimneys while a fire was burning in the grate!

After the move, keep the cat in the house for about five days and keep a close eye on it when it does eventually go outside. Most cats are timid about new territory and will not venture far until they are more confident but there are stories of cats that have made long and gruelling journeys to arrive, thin and foot-

sore, on the doorstep of their old home months later. Don't bother to daub your cat's paws with butter: it doesn't work and will only make a mess of your furniture.

THE LOST CAT

Thousands of cats go missing every year: some are adopted by other families, some are killed on the roads, some inadvertently take a ride in a lorry, some are abducted. Others eventually wander home by themselves but your best chance of finding a lost cat is leaving no stone unturned. Once you have searched *everywhere* at home - that includes refrigerator, deep freeze, washing machine and drawers - ask all the neighbours to check sheds and garages. Once you are certain that the cat has gone, notify veterinarians and animal rescue centres within a 24km (15 mile) radius. Draw up posters to fix on trees and circulars to deliver around the neighbourhood - try delivering one to the first house on either side of each road, asking the occupants to pass it on. Offer as big a reward as you can.

BELOW: *During a house move, keep the cat confined until all the activity is over and keep a close eye on it once it is released.*

Chapter 8
HEALTH CARE

Cats may show few symptoms in the early stages of an illness and in a busy household,

these are easily overlooked. The secret of good cat care is knowing your pet's habits

and keeping a close eye if they change in any way.

If you notice any of the following symptoms you should take your cat to the veterinarian immediately:

★ Excessive thirst.
★ Marked changes in eating patterns: the cat is off its food or is eating much more than usual for more than 24 hours.
★ Straining in the litter tray.
★ Generally dull and listless appearance.
★ Noticeable weight loss.
★ Bleeding from the mouth, anus or genitals.

Other symptoms may not be so clear-cut. Many a healthy cat will vomit or sneeze occasionally, without the need for a panic visit to the veterinarian. The chart below gives general guidelines on the action you should take but the golden rule is that if you are unhappy about your cat's condition or demeanour, contact the veterinarian without delay.

LEFT: *A visit to the veterinarian for a check-up in the first few months of life will reassure that all is well.*

VOMITING

WHAT TO CHECK	WHAT TO DO
Has the cat been grooming itself and is it bringing up fur? Is the cat bringing up undigested food?	If no other worrying signs, give no food overnight, then feed a light meal.
Is there any blood in the vomit? Does the cat have other signs of illness (eg diarrhoea, lethargy, dull looks)?	Consult your veterinarian without delay. Digestive disorders can be serious.

DIARRHOEA

WHAT TO CHECK	WHAT TO DO
Have you given the cat extra milk, or fed cow's milk to a kitten?	If the cat seems well otherwise, give no food overnight, then give a light meal.
Have you changed the cat's diet?	If the problem does not recur, there is no need to worry.
Is there blood in the faeces?	Consult your veterinarian without delay.
Does the cat have any other signs of illness (eg vomiting, lethargy, dull looks)?	Digestive disorders can be serious.

COUGHING/SNEEZING

WHAT TO CHECK	WHAT TO DO
Is the room full of cigarette smoke? Have you sprayed with insecticide, air freshener etc.? Has the cat been poking in dusty corners?	Dust or air the room for the sake of both cats and humans.
Does the cat have any other symptoms: runny nose, eye discharge etc. Does the cough sound dry and hacking? Does the cough sound phlegmy? Is the cough or sneezing persistent?	Consult the veterinarian without delay: this may be an infection or an allergic reaction. Give no medication advice.

TAKING YOUR CAT'S TEMPERATURE

This is a two-person job. Ask your helper to hold the cat by the scruff of the neck, with another hand under the body, behind the hind legs. Use a small-bulbed clinical thermometer, the end greased with vegetable oil and shake down the mercury. Lift the cat's tail and insert the thermometer slowly but firmly into the cat's rectum until about one third is inside the cat. Hold it in place for one minute then remove and wipe it before reading. Normal temperature varies between 38° and 39°C (100° and 102°F)

SCRATCHING

WHAT TO CHECK	WHAT TO DO
Are there black specks visible in the cat's fur? Is there any sign of dry, scaly patches?	Use flea powder or spray: follow manufacturer's instructions exactly. Consult your veterinarian immediately.
Are there any bald patches?	Your cat probably has a skin disorder.
Do you live in the country? If so, check for small, bluish swellings.	These are probably sheep ticks. Ask your vet to remove them; partial removal can lead to abscesses.
Is the cat scratching its ears? Is there any dark brown wax visible?	Ear mites are very common; your veterinarian will prescribe ear drops.

URINARY PROBLEMS

WHAT TO CHECK	WHAT TO DO
Is a normally clean cat urinating in the wrong place and is there any blood in the urine? Is the cat straining in the litter tray? Is the cat constantly licking its hindparts?	Consult your veterinarian immediately. This may be cystitis or the more serious feline urological syndrome.
Is your cat urinating more frequently and drinking a lot? Is it losing weight? Does it have bad breath?	Chronic kidney disease is common as a cat grows older. Consult your veterinarian; early treatment will be beneficial.

MAKING THE MOST OF YOUR VETERINARIAN

In most areas, there is no shortage of veterinary surgeons but not all veterinarians are equally good with all animals. Ask among local cat owners – or better still, cat breeders – to find the best cat veterinarian. When you first acquire your cat, take it along for a checkup, even if it does not need injections, so that the vet knows your cat and has its details recorded before you have to hurry along with a problem. Ask whether he or she is willing to make house calls, if necessary, and what arrangements are made for 24 hour emergency cover.

When you take your cat for a consultation, note down any symptoms, any alteration in eating and drinking habits, anything unusual you have seen in the litter tray and any changes in behaviour you have noticed. The more information you can give, the easier it will be for the veterinarian to make an informed diagnosis.

BELOW: *When a cat starts scratching repeatedly, check the condition of skin and fur for any symptoms.*

ANCHORING A CAT

Cats are notoriously difficult to hold in position for examination or treatment; they can wriggle, squirm and kick their way free if not held in the right way. If the cat is lying down, it may be sufficient to hold it by the shoulders with one hand on either side of the body or, if it is sitting down, hold it gently by the scruff with one hand, while the other is round its chest. If the cat is making a determined effort to escape, then hold it firmly by the scruff and by its front legs.

Administering eye or ear treatment to a panicky cat can be a tricky business, so use a thick towel or small blanket. Holding the cat by the scruff all the time, place it on the towel, then wrap it up so that only its head is free. Move quickly and firmly without being rough. The cat is then unable to wriggle or scratch and many cats calm down quickly in this position. You will still need to hold the cat but it will struggle much less as you administer treatment or make an examination.

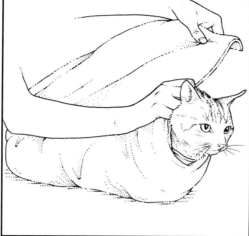

1 Hold the cat by the shoulders with one hand on each side of the body.

2 Place the cat on the towel and wrap tightly.

3 Tuck in the edge of the towel, leaving the head free ready for treatment.

NURSING A SICK CAT

A sick cat needs a quiet place in a warm, draught-free but well-ventilated location. A large, high-sided cardboard box with a 'door' cut in the front will provide a snug bed which can be replaced as often as necessary. Line the box with newspaper and towels and provide a luke-warm hot water bottle, carefully wrapped, in one corner. Find the time to give your cat a gentle massage regularly, concentrating particularly on its legs and paws. This is relaxing and beneficial when the cat is depressed.

Your cat may not be interested in eating, but tempt it with small, frequent meals of cooked fish or poultry, scrambled egg or meat and fish-based baby foods and serve food warmed to blood temperature. If your cat has an illness that affects its sense of smell, try strong-smelling dishes, like pilchards. Though a cat can go without food for quite a long time, dehydration can be a

MASSAGING PAWS

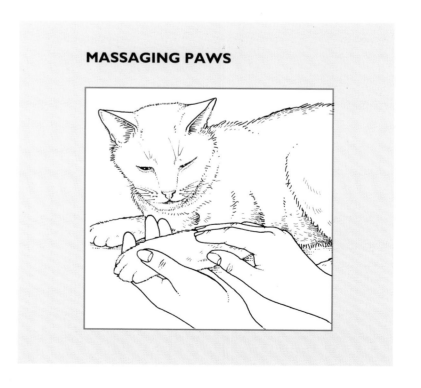

GIVING A PILL

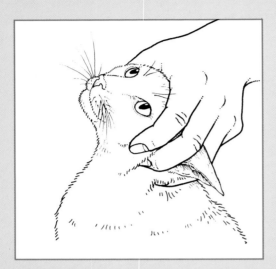

STEP 1 Place your left hand over the cat's temples, without touching its whiskers, and raise its head slightly, meanwhile pressing its jaws gently with your thumb and index finger.

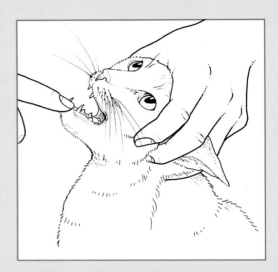

STEP 2 With the index finger of your right hand, press lightly on the front of the cat's mouth to open it. Talk soothingly to your cat all the time.

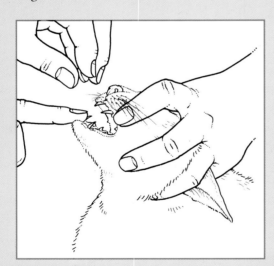

STEP 3 Ask a helper to put the pill at the base of the cat's tongue and give it a slight push. The pill may go down more easily if you smear it with butter first.

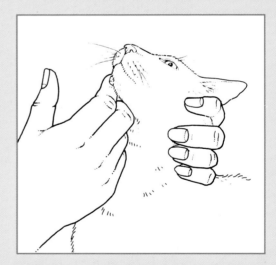

STEP 4 Close the cat's mouth but if it does not swallow immediately, keep its head back and stroke its throat until it does swallow.

problem, and can become dangerous if the cat is losing fluid through vomiting and diarrhoea. Your veterinarian may advise you to limit the cat's intake to liquidized meals, or fish and meat juices, which can be fed by syringe. Anchor the cat to make this process easier.

When using a syringe, hold the head as you would for giving a pill, then insert the syringe between the teeth at the side of the cat's mouth. The liquid should then be dribbled in, a few drops at a time. Go slowly, or it may go down the wrong way, and pause after every two or three drops so that the cat can swallow.

If its nose is blocked up, it will also need time to breathe! Some cats will not accept syringe feeding and in this case, your veterinarian may have to administer a drip.

While your cat is sick, you may need to keep its face clean by wiping away any discharge from around the eyes, nose or mouth. Use a clean pad of cotton wool, dampened with fresh warm water, for each area. If there is diarrhoea, you will need to clean its rear end as well.

EMERGENCY ACTION

In an emergency, you will want to get your cat to the veterinarian as quickly as possible, but you may need to administer first aid in the meantime. Never give your cat medicine meant for humans or other animals and don't give an injured cat anything to eat or drink before seeing the veterinarian, as he may need to give an anaesthetic. Remember that if it is frightened or in pain, your normally affectionate cat may turn on you and inflict injuries, so if possible wear a pair of gloves or have a coat or blanket ready to wrap round the cat if necessary.

Resuscitation
Only attempt to resuscitate a cat if you are absolutely certain that its breathing or heart has stopped and getting professional help would take too long. There may be an occasion where

ADMINISTERING EAR DROPS

First clean dirt and wax from the outer folds of the ear with damp cotton wool but don't attempt to poke inside (right). Hold the outer ear flap back and tilt the cat's head slightly sideways (below left). Allow the liquid to drip into the ear canal and hold the head steady for long enough to allow it to penetrate. Gently massage the cat's ear, then clean away any excess liquid (below right).

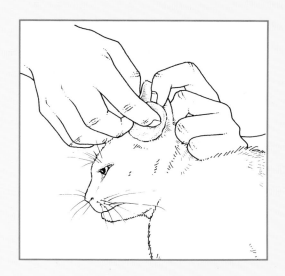

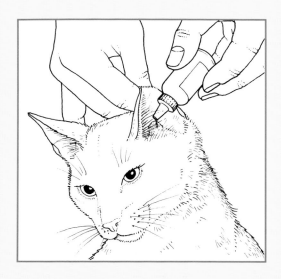

APPLYING EYE DROPS/OINTMENT

When applying eye drops or ointment, hold the cat's head steady with a hand across the temples, but do not tilt it backwards. Drops should be applied from above; ointment should be applied so that a small amount falls across the eyeball. Hold the eyelids together for a few moments before you release the cat.

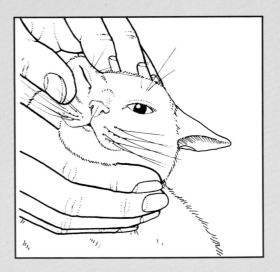

ARTIFICIAL RESPIRATION

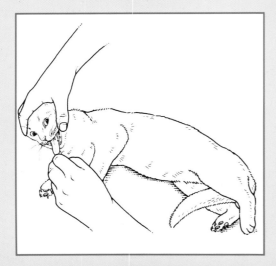

Before beginning artificial respiration, extend the cat's head and pull out it's tongue. Sometimes this action alone will re-start breathing.

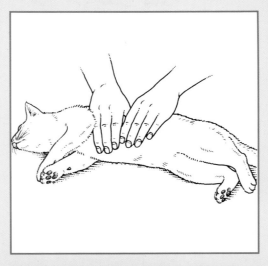

If the cat does not breathe, lay both hands on its ribs, press gently, and then release quickly. Repeat every five seconds.

MOUTH-TO-MOUTH RESUSCITATION

Mouth-to-mouth resuscitation for a cat applies the same principles as the human 'kiss-of-life' and is probably the best method to use if you are not sure what injuries the cat has sustained. Amateur first-aiders using more aggressive methods may run the risk of doing more harm than good. Always remember that resuscitation techniques are only for use in an emergency; get professional help whenever possible.

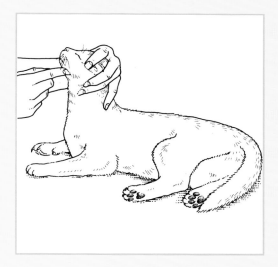

1 First, extend the head and check that the airway is clear.

2 Cup hands over the cat's nose and open mouth.

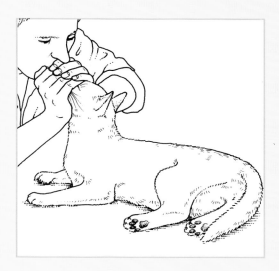

3 Blow in air for three seconds. Pause for two seconds, then repeat.

your actions are the only chance of saving the cat's life but never forget that amateur resuscitation attempts may cause more damage to an injured animal so they must only be used in dire emergency. If possible, ask someone to telephone the veterinarian while you begin resuscitation.

If the cat has stopped breathing but its heart is still beating, keep it lying flat and check that its mouth and throat are unobstructed. Remove any foreign bodies, wipe away any blood or vomit. Extend the cat's head and pull out its tongue – in some cases, this alone will re-start breathing. Place the palm of your hand on the ribs, with your other hand on top. Press gently, then release immediately. Repeat at five second intervals. An alternative method is mouth-to-mouth resuscitation, which should be used if you suspect that the cat might have chest damage – for instance, after a car accident. Raise the cat's head, cup your hands over its nose, and blow in air for three seconds. Pause for two seconds, then repeat.

If the cat's heart has stopped (you can check for heartbeat by placing your fingertips on the lower part of the chest, behind the front elbow) check airways and extend the tongue as above. Place both hands in the middle of the chest and press gently but firmly for a count of two. Release for a count of two and repeat six times. Alternate with artificial respiration and continue. During both procedures **BE GENTLE**. Remember that you could easily damage the cat's ribs.

Moving an injured cat

In many cases an injured cat, whether conscious or not, will have to be moved for safety's sake. If it is unconscious, make sure that its airway is clear, as described above. Lay a coat or blanket alongside the cat, then with one hand under its chest and the other under its rump, slide it onto the blanket, keeping its body as straight as possible. It should be handled as little as possible in case it has internal injuries or broken limbs. If you have help, then two people can carry the blanket with a hand at each corner, keeping the cat's body flat. If you are alone, carry it like a hammock. Obviously it is best if you can put the cat into a large box or carrier and cover its body warmly. If you have to lay it on the back seat of the car, try to enlist a helper who can sit with it, in case it comes round and needs to be anchored or restrained in some way while in the car. It may be advisable to keep the cat basket on hand in case the cat panics. If the cat is conscious and panicky, approach it from behind, hold it by the scruff of the neck and wrap it quickly in a coat or blanket, making sure that its paws are enclosed. Don't hesitate: a frightened and injured cat may follow its instincts and bolt, perhaps to die alone for want of treatment. If you suspect that one of its limbs is injured, avoid touching it and when you put the cat in its carrier, make sure that the limb is uppermost. Don't attempt to apply a splint to a broken limb; you may do more harm than good.

BLEEDING

If the only injury is a minor graze, clean it with a pad of damp cotton wool, trim away any matted hair and apply a mild antiseptic. A minor wound can be cleansed in the same way, then covered with an absorbent pad (not cotton wool) and secured with a bandage or with adhesive tape, wound round the limb or body so that it will stick to itself.

Stop the bleeding from a serious wound using a gauze pad (or a clean handkerchief in an emergency) soaked in cold water and applying pressure for two or three minutes. Then bandage over the pad and take the cat straight to the veterinarian.

MOVING AN UNCONSCIOUS CAT

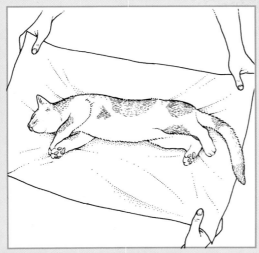

If possible, two people should carry the blanket, to keep the cat's body flat.

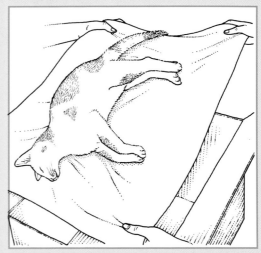

Put the cat, still lying flat into a large box or carrier, then cover it's body warmly.

ABOVE: *Play fighting like this rarely results in injury but if the skin is grazed, ensure that the wound is kept clean.*

When the burn comes from chemicals, keep pouring clean water over the site to wash off the substance. If you are certain that the chemical is acid (battery acid, for example), you can use a weak solution of sodium bicarbonate and if you are sure that it

Never apply a bandage too tightly or you may affect the cat's circulation.

BURNS

In the case of a burn on the paw, hold it under a running tap for several minutes. If the burn is elsewhere, apply an ice pack made from ice cubes in a plastic bag, wrapped in a clean cloth (a packet of frozen peas can make a useful substitute). For a minor burn, apply petroleum jelly; otherwise take your cat to the veterinarian.

FIRST AID KIT

Thermometer
Safe disinfectant
Blunt-ended scissors
Tweezers
Gauze pads
Cotton wool
Cotton wool buds
Bandages (various widths)
Antiseptic cream (specially formulated for cats)
Petroleum jelly

BANDAGING A BLEEDING PAW

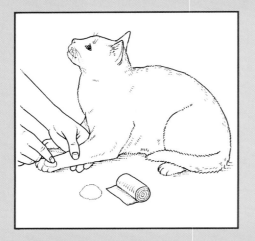
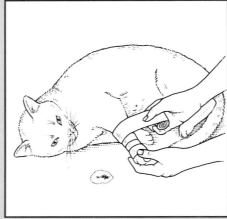
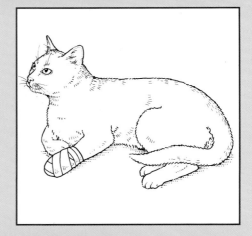

Clean the wound with a pad of damp cotton wool and apply antiseptic.

Apply a soft, absorbent pad to the wound and bandage firmly.

Fasten the end of the bandage securely and keep cat calm and quiet.

REMOVING A FOREIGN OBJECT FROM THE THROAT WITH TWEEZERS

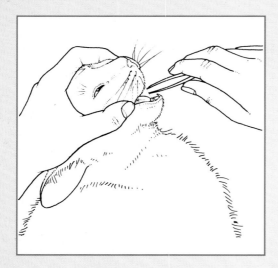

If you can see the object, take a pair of tweezers in one hand and, holding the cat's mouth with the other hand, gently extract the foreign body

is alkaline (ammonia or caustic soda, for instance) you can use a weak vinegar solution.

CHOKING

Occasionally a cat may get a bone or other foreign body stuck in its throat and begin choking and gasping for air. Restrain the cat, wrapping it in a towel if necessary, and open its mouth as you would when giving a pill. Look down the throat (a small torch will be useful) and if you can see the object, try to remove it with tweezers. If you can't see the object and reach it easily, don't poke around as you may cause tissue damage. Try turning the cat upside down and giving it a firm shake but if this does not work, get the cat to the veterinarian as quickly as possible.

STINGS

If your cat has been stung, cut away a little of the fur surrounding the swelling. If you see a black bee sting, remove it with tweezers, then apply antiseptic or bathe it in a cold sodium bicarbonate solution. Bathe a wasp sting with a vinegar solution.

A sting in the mouth can be dangerous, as the swelling can lead to breathing difficulties, so consult a veterinarian without delay.

INSURANCE

Many companies offer insurance for cats, and you will probably be able to pick up a handful of leaflets from your veterinary surgery. Terms vary, so compare details carefully: some plans offer little more than cover for veterinary treatment, others offer a range of benefits from replacement costs if your cat dies or goes missing to the cost of boarding cats if you are hospitalized. Calculate the costs carefully when deciding whether to insure: if you would not be able to afford the cost of treatment if your cat was seriously ill or injured, then insurance may give you peace of mind. On the other hand, remember that insurance will not cover the cost of preventative treatment, such as inoculations, or expenses connected with neutering or kitten-

ing. In addition, you will normally have to pay, on current prices, the first £25 or so of every claim for veterinary treatment – and this is more than the cost of a visit to the veterinarian for a minor problem. You may think that an indoor cat is far less at risk of accident or disease than an outdoor roamer, so the cost of premiums is less worthwhile.

BELOW: *A contented cat in the peak of good health is a joy to see and a credit to its owner.*

INDEX